I ♥ mom

Rachael Tarfman-Perez

Alaya books

The world needs your story.

Copyright © 2023 Rachael Tarfman-Perez
All rights reserved. No part of this book may be reproduced or used in any manner without written permission of the copyright owner except for the use of quotations in a book review.

First Edition printed April 2023
Created by Rachael Tarfman-Perez
Internal design by Lezanne Swart

Cover design by Aleksandra Koleśniak
www.rachaeltarfmanperez.com

Published by Alaya Books
www.alayabooks.com

The world needs your story.

♥ ♥ ♥

To all of the fabulous moms in the world.
Never underestimate your worth - you are loved
and appreciated more than you know.

"Mommy when you're a kid
and I'm a grown up, I am going
to pick you up from your daycare
and Mommy you can go
to sleep with me,
you are my best friend."

Julius, Age 2
Munich, Germany

"I love my mummy because when I am crying she makes me feel better and because she made me a Halloween birthday party."

Katia Age 3
Barcelona, Spain

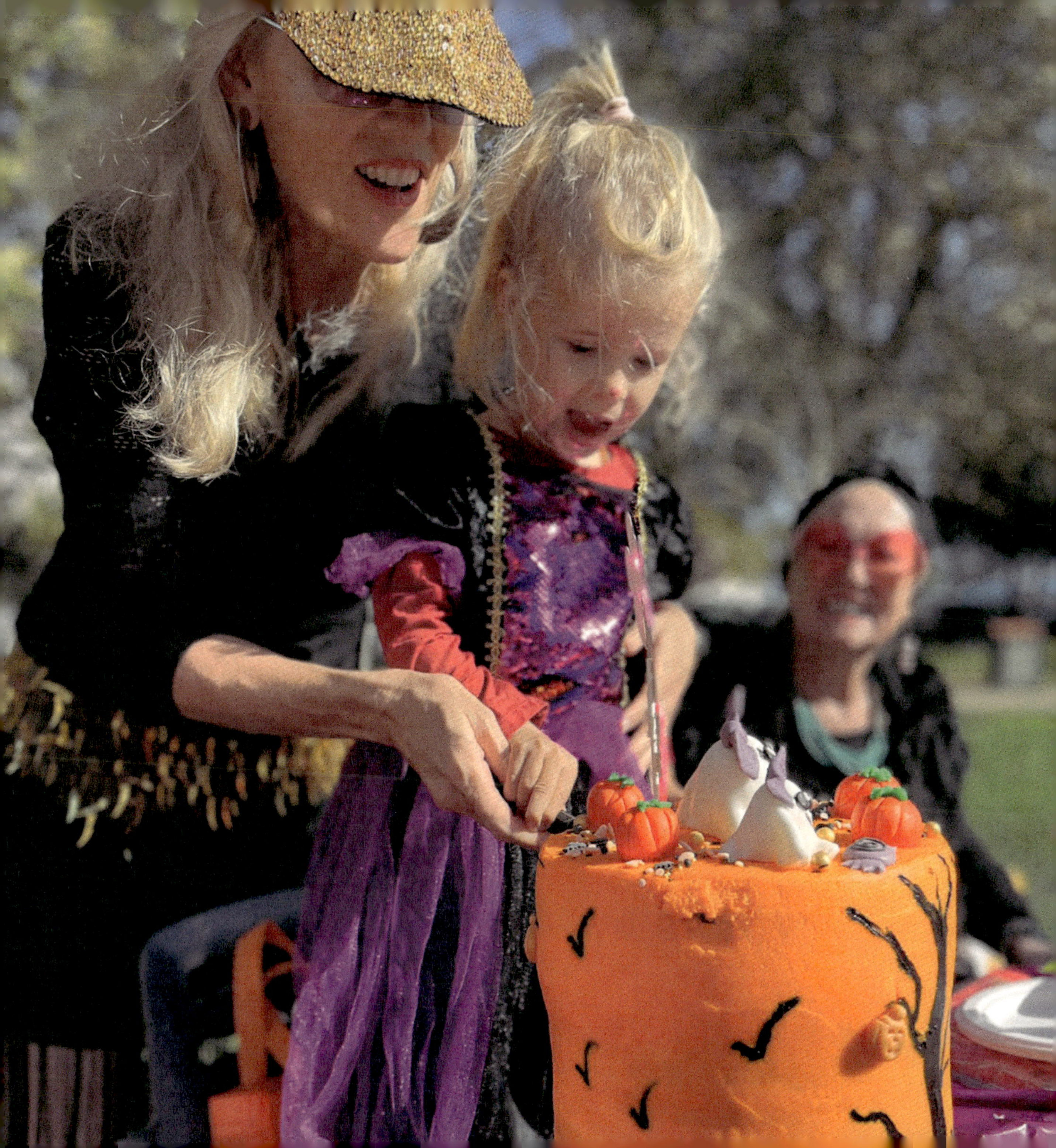

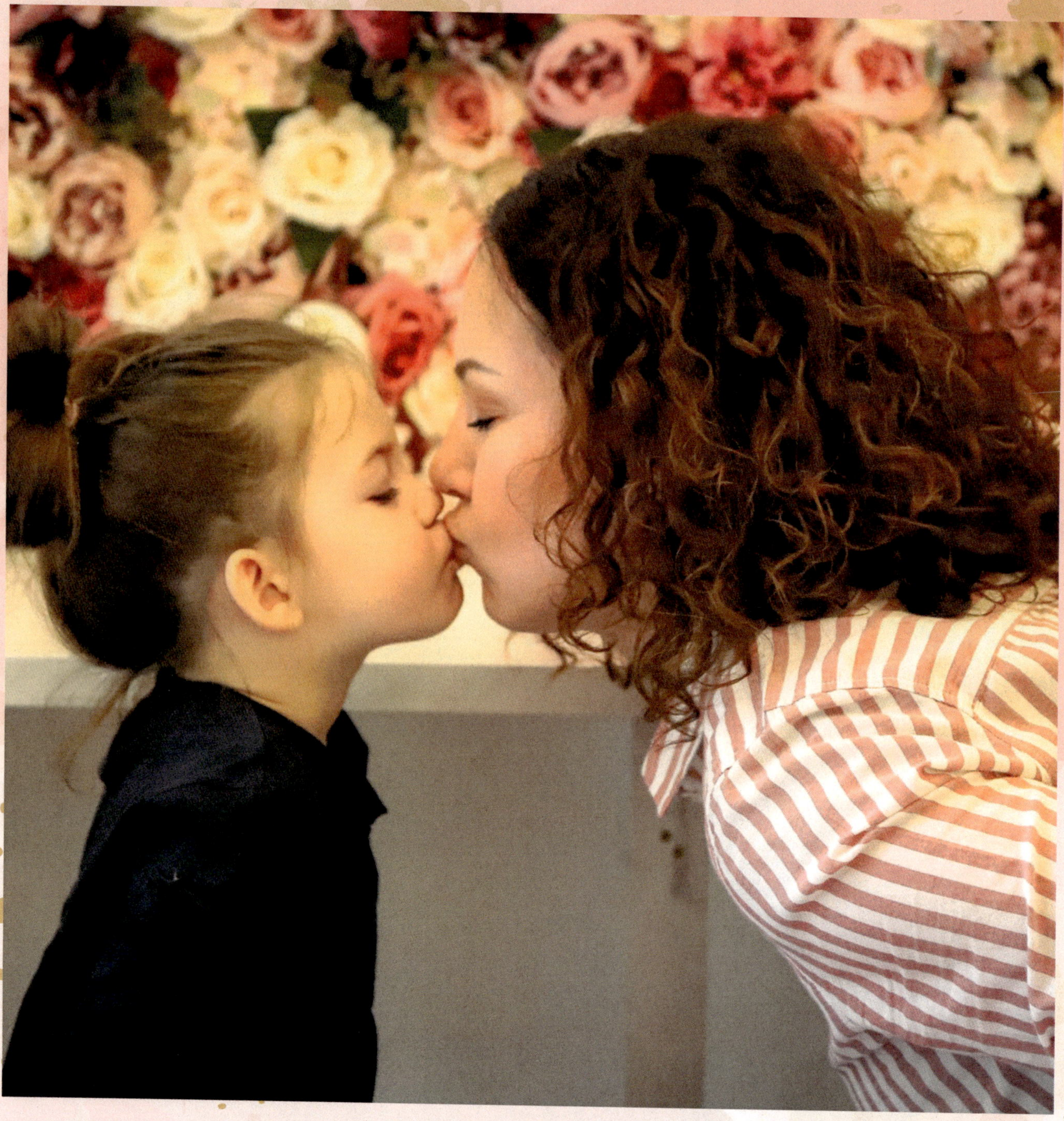

"I love my mummy because she makes me nice food and is beautiful."

Lyla, Age 3
Yorkshire, UK

"Do you know what is
the biggest number?
A hundred. Mama,
I love you a hundred!"

Alicia, Age 4
Biarritz, France

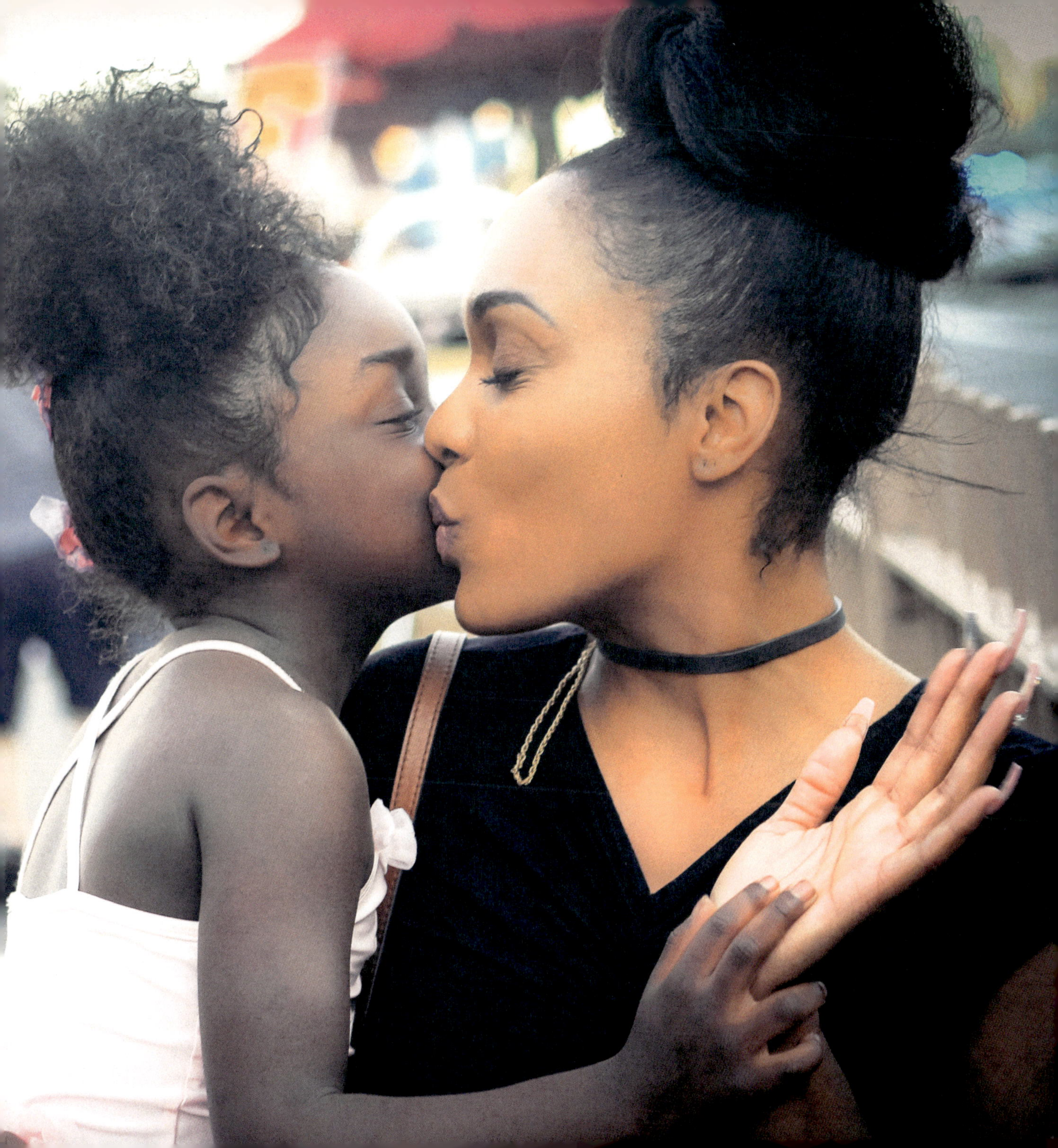

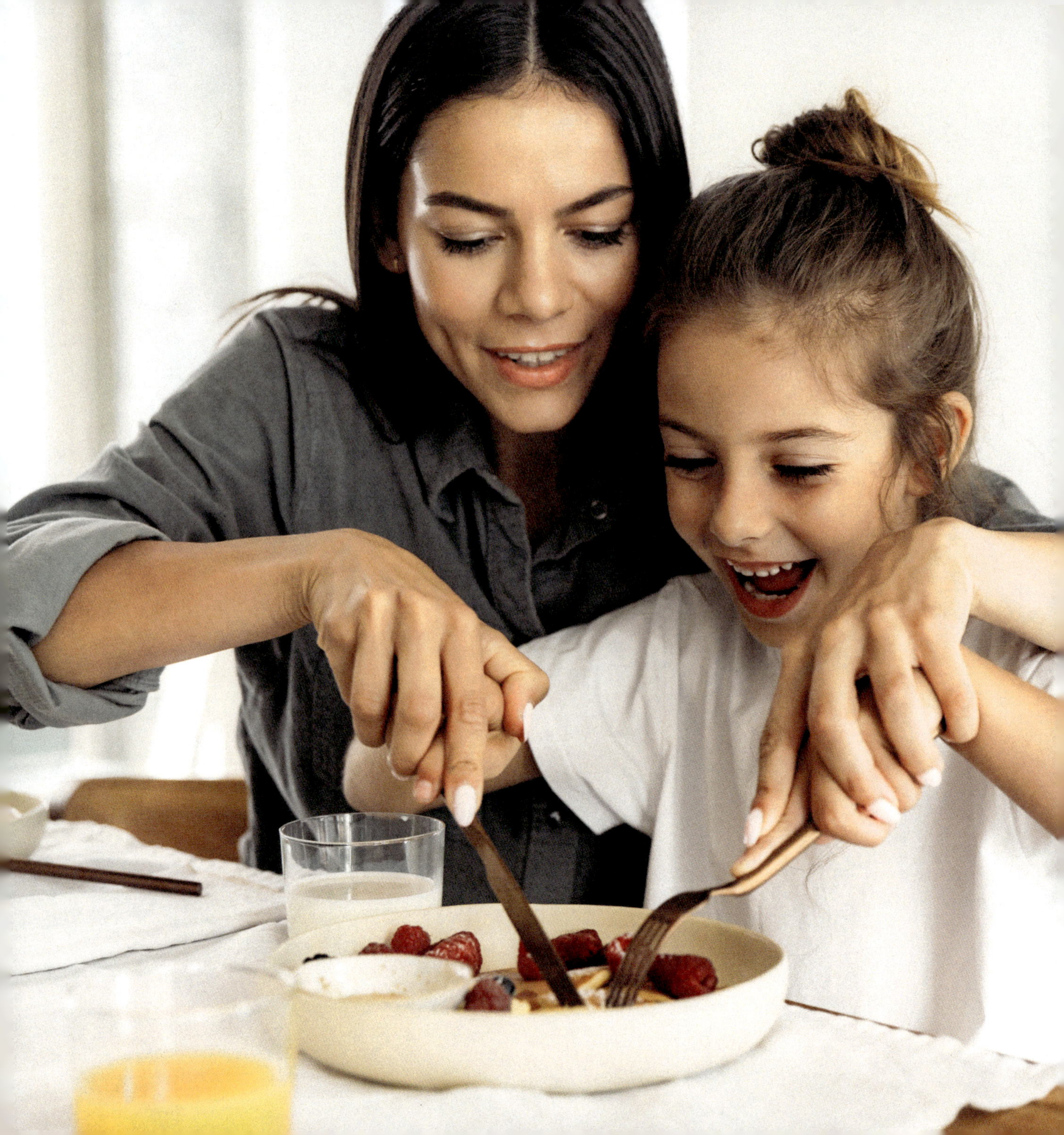

"What I love most about my mom is that she gives me breakfast."

Atarah, Age 4
Bakersfield, California

"What I love most about my mom
is that she gives me food,
plays with me and she is sweet."

Jasmine, Age 4
Orange County, California

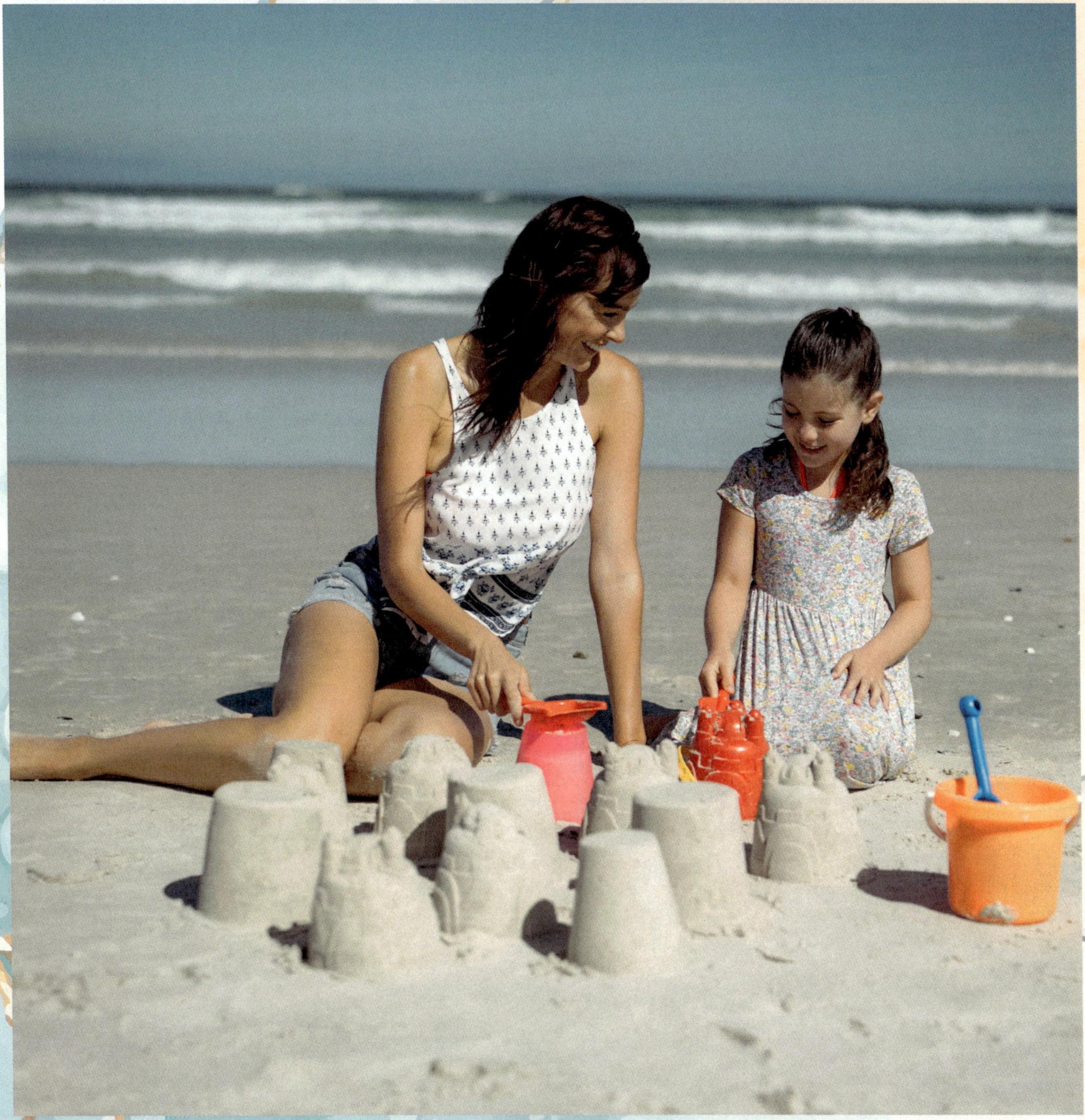

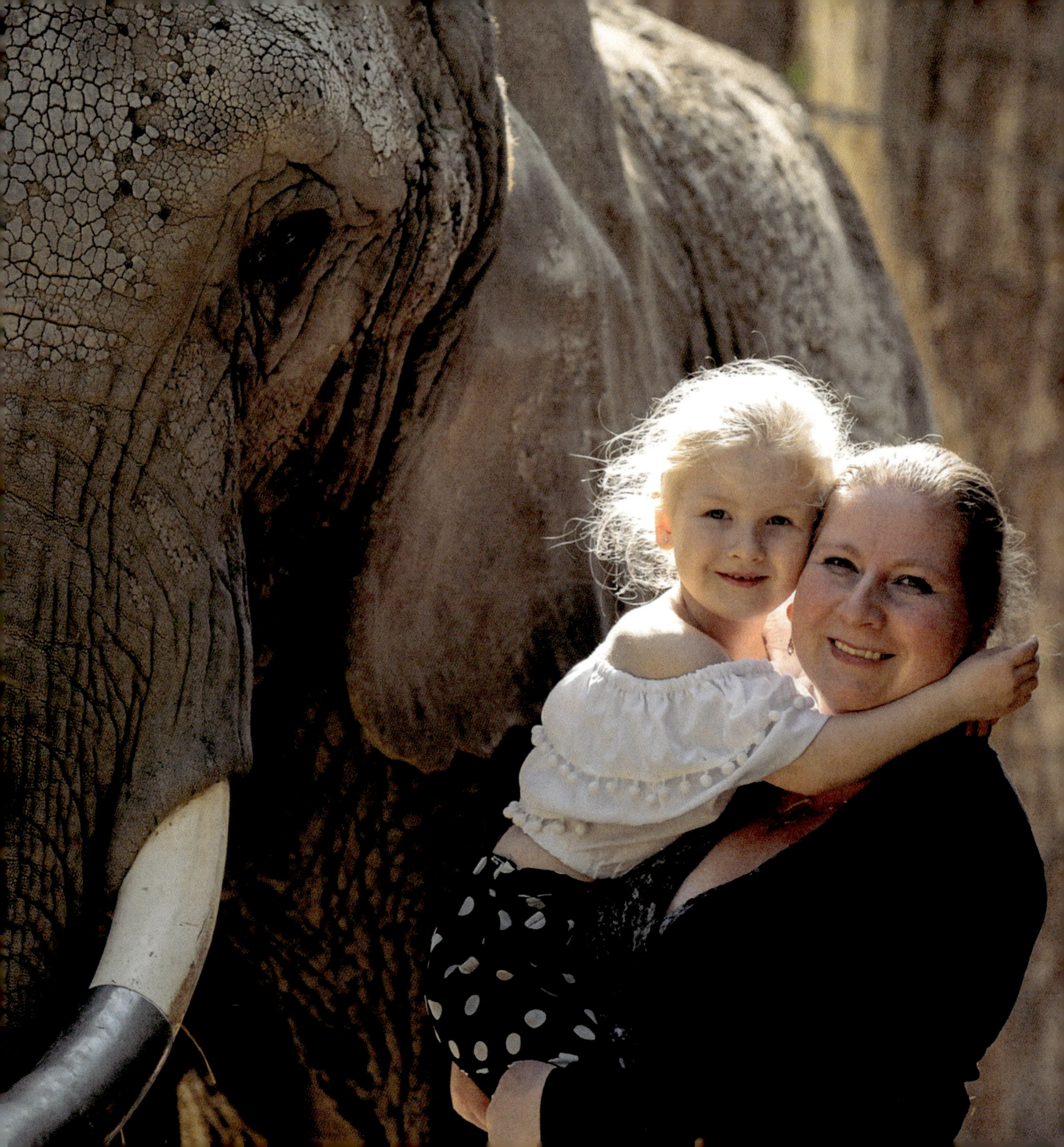

"What I love about my mum is that sometimes she lets me do what I want to do."

Nahla, Age 4
Weisbaden, Germany

"I love my mummy because
she reads me nice stories at bedtime
and does nice things for me
like taking me to the forest,
and giving me sweets and treats."

Summer, Age 4
Yorkshire, United Kingdom

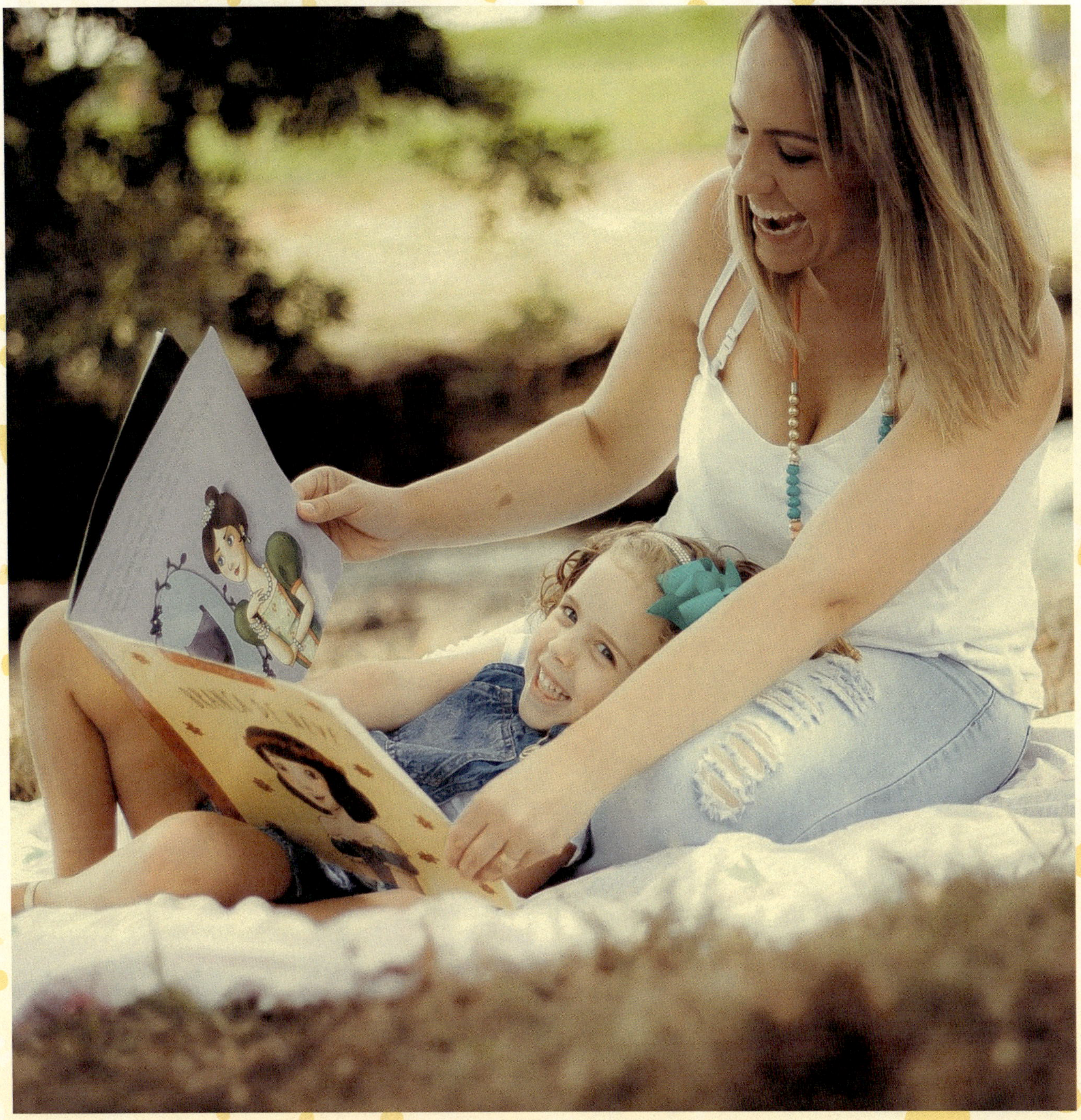

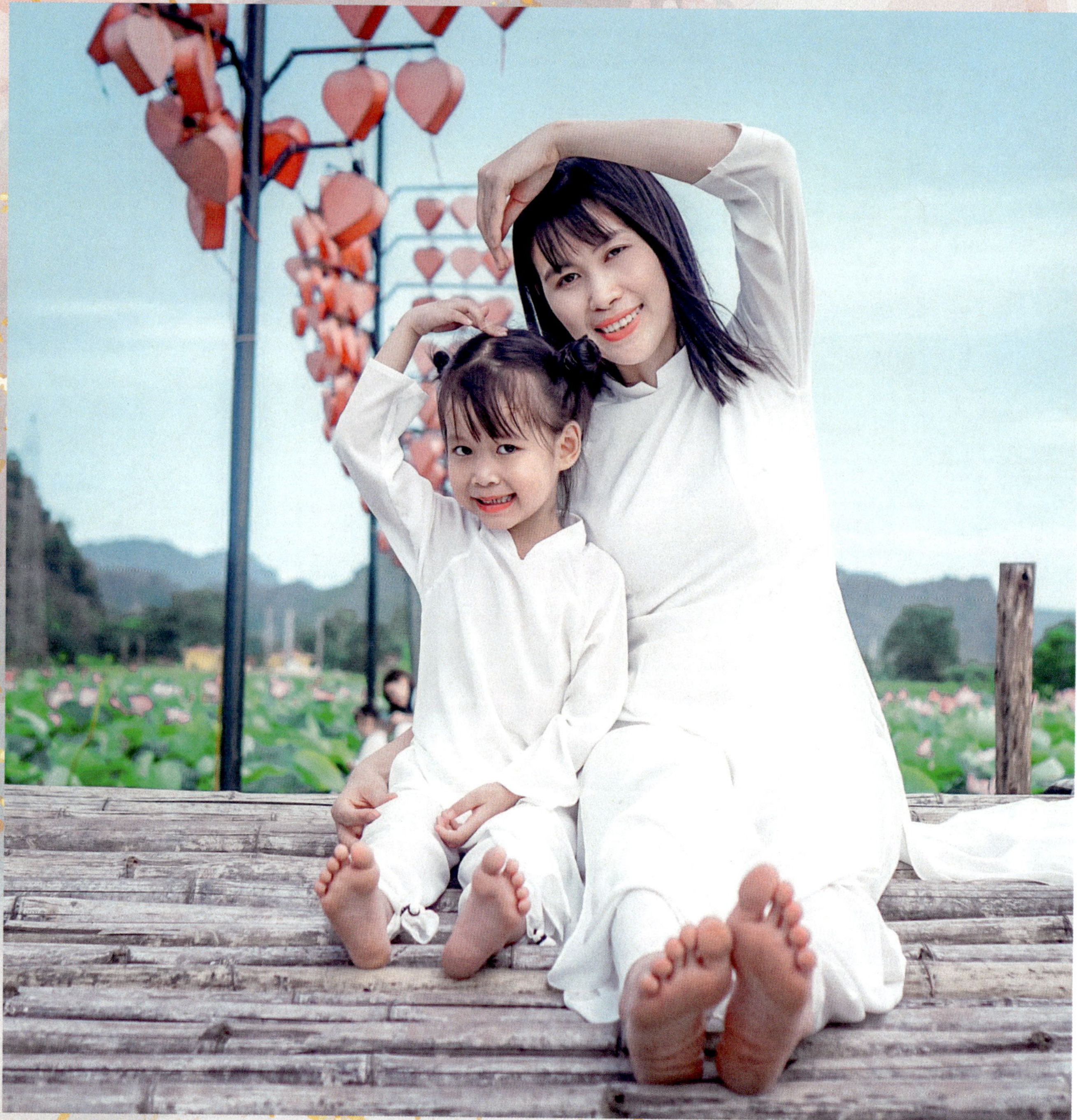

"I love my mama because she is grateful and she buys me a Pokemon Eevee."

Penelope, Age 5
Bangkok, Thailand

"What I love about my mum is she is kind and helpful and loving and peaceful."

Miles, Age 5
Hertfordshire, United Kingdom

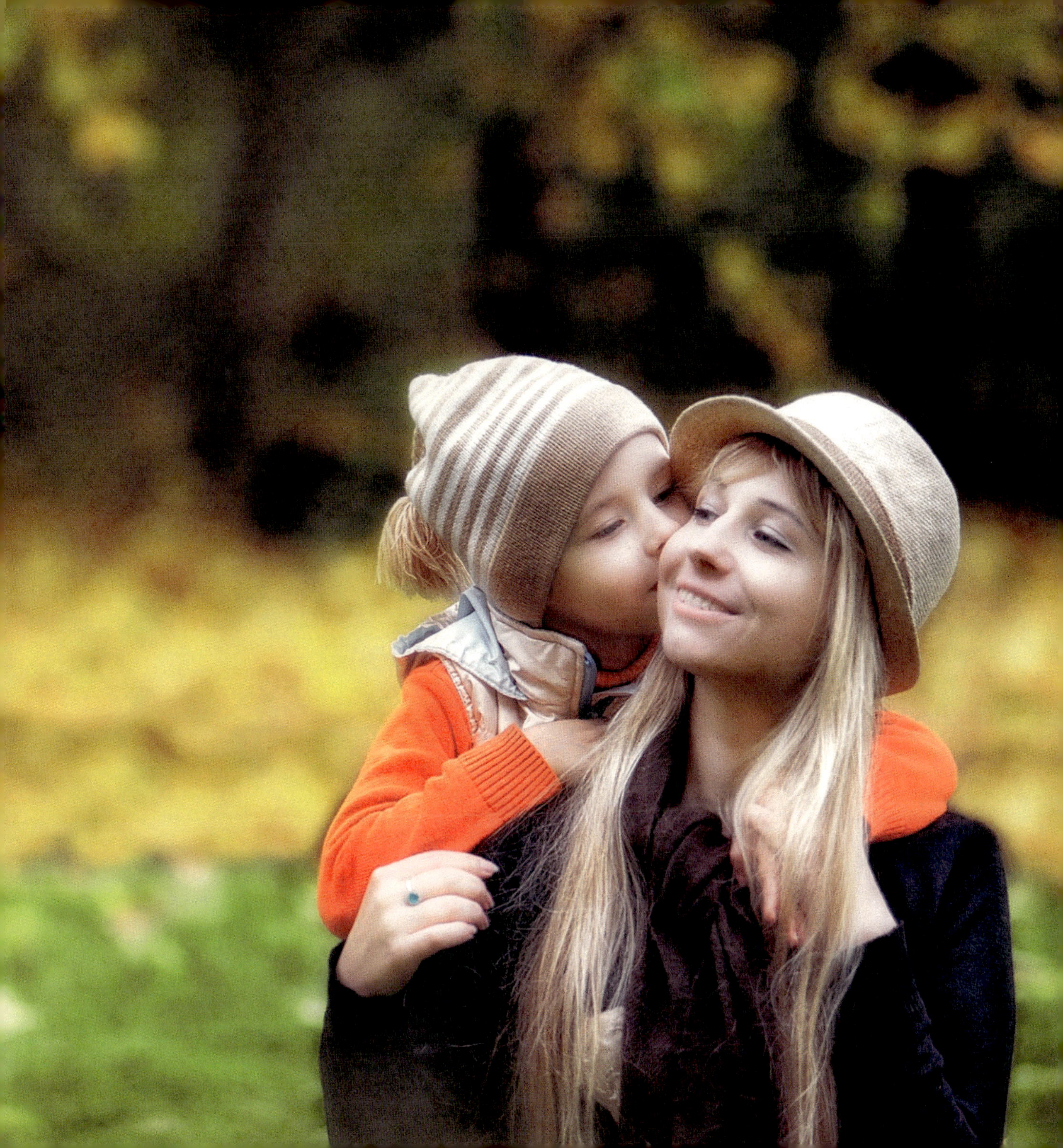

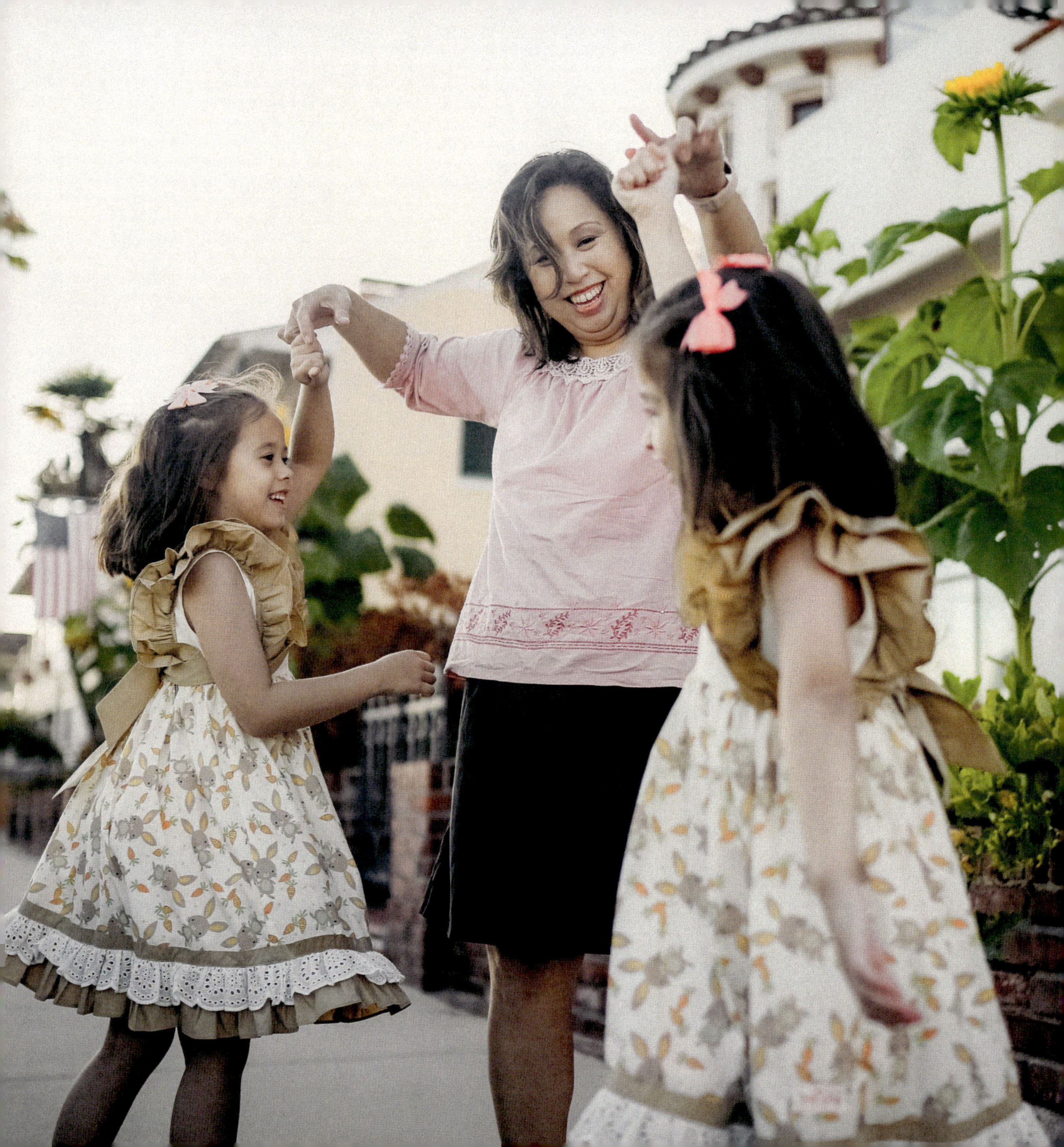

"I love my mama because she is pretty as a princess. I love how she makes my hair and that we dance together."

Lara, Age 5
Mexico City, Mexico

"I like my Mummy because she gives me lots of cuddles and kisses. Because she makes me yummy food and because she gave me a puppy."

Isabelle, Age 5
Dubai, United Arab Emirates

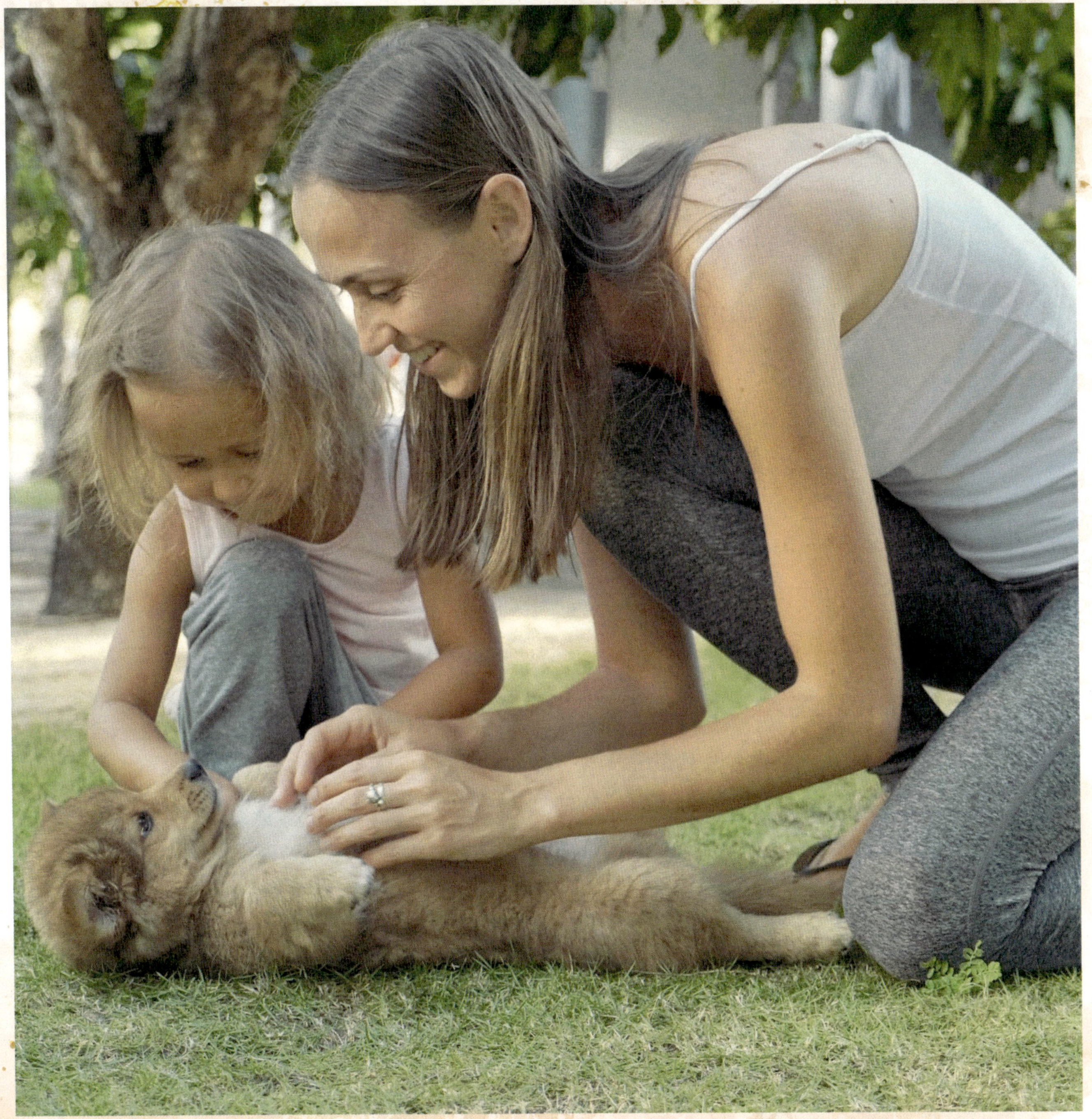

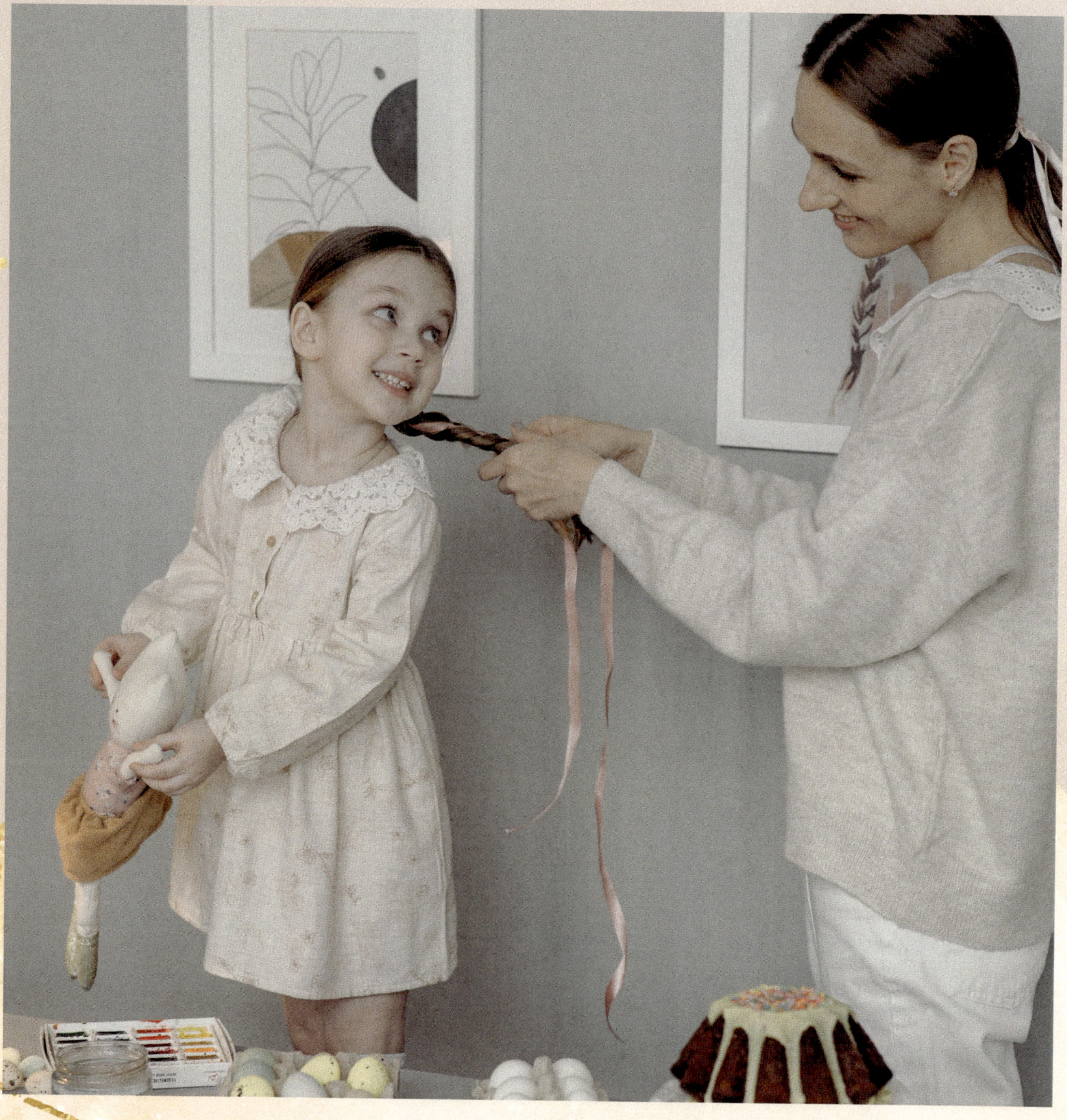

"What I love about my mum is to be with her always and that she helps me with so many things like braiding my hair and giving me a new soft toy."

Melissa, Age 5
Gothenburg, Sweden

*"I love my mom because
she has the best hugs
and her smile feels like sunshine
on a cold, difficult day."*

Catherine, Age 6
Cape Town, South Africa

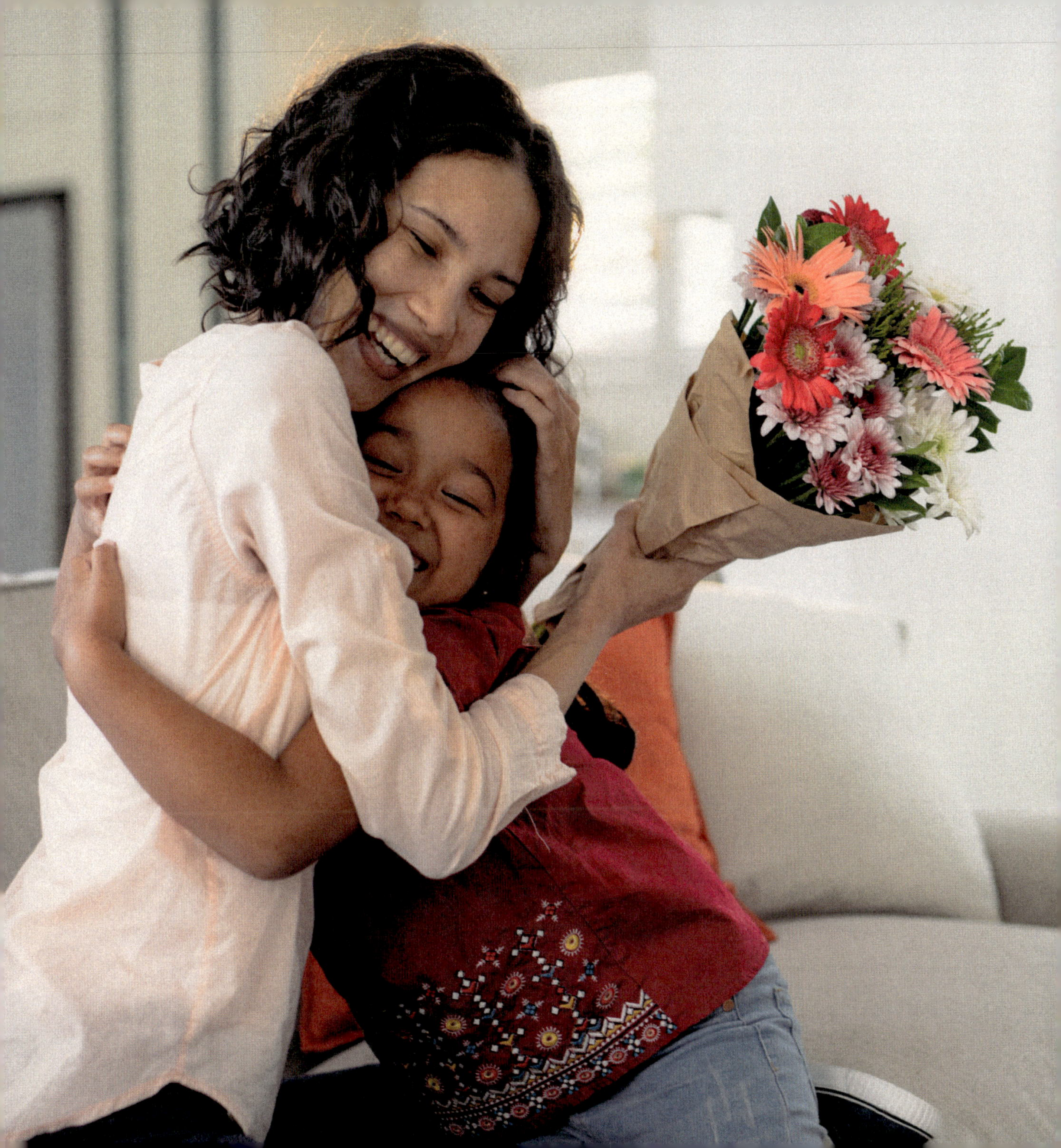

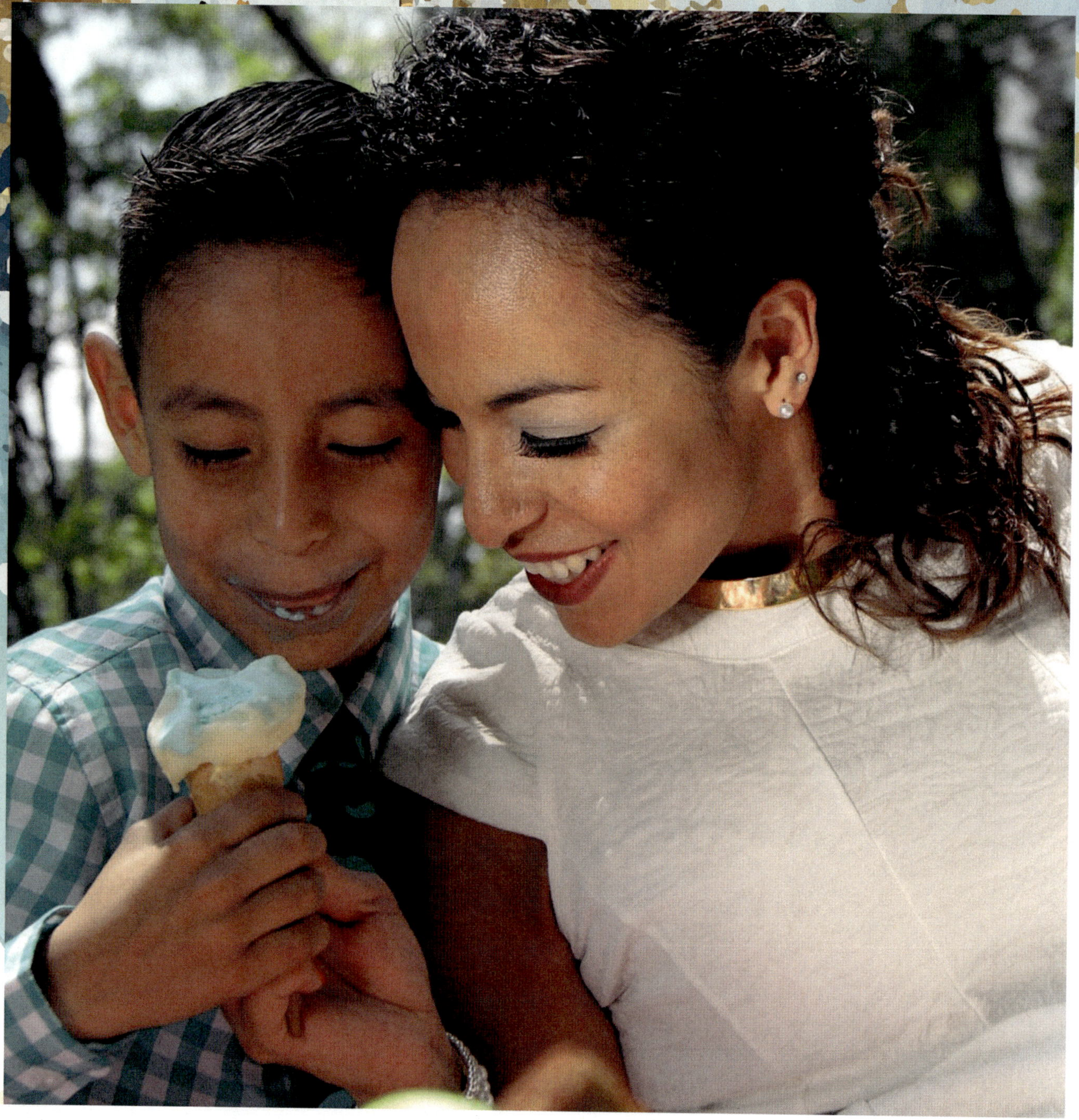

"What I love about my mum is that
she loves me with all her heart
and always helps me with my problems.
She's really nice to me,
she makes me laugh,
and we do fun things together."

Leonard, Age 7
Barcelona, Spain

"What I love about my mum is that I get to hug her a lot and I also get to see her a lot because she is my mum."

Aria, Age 7
Melbourne, Australia

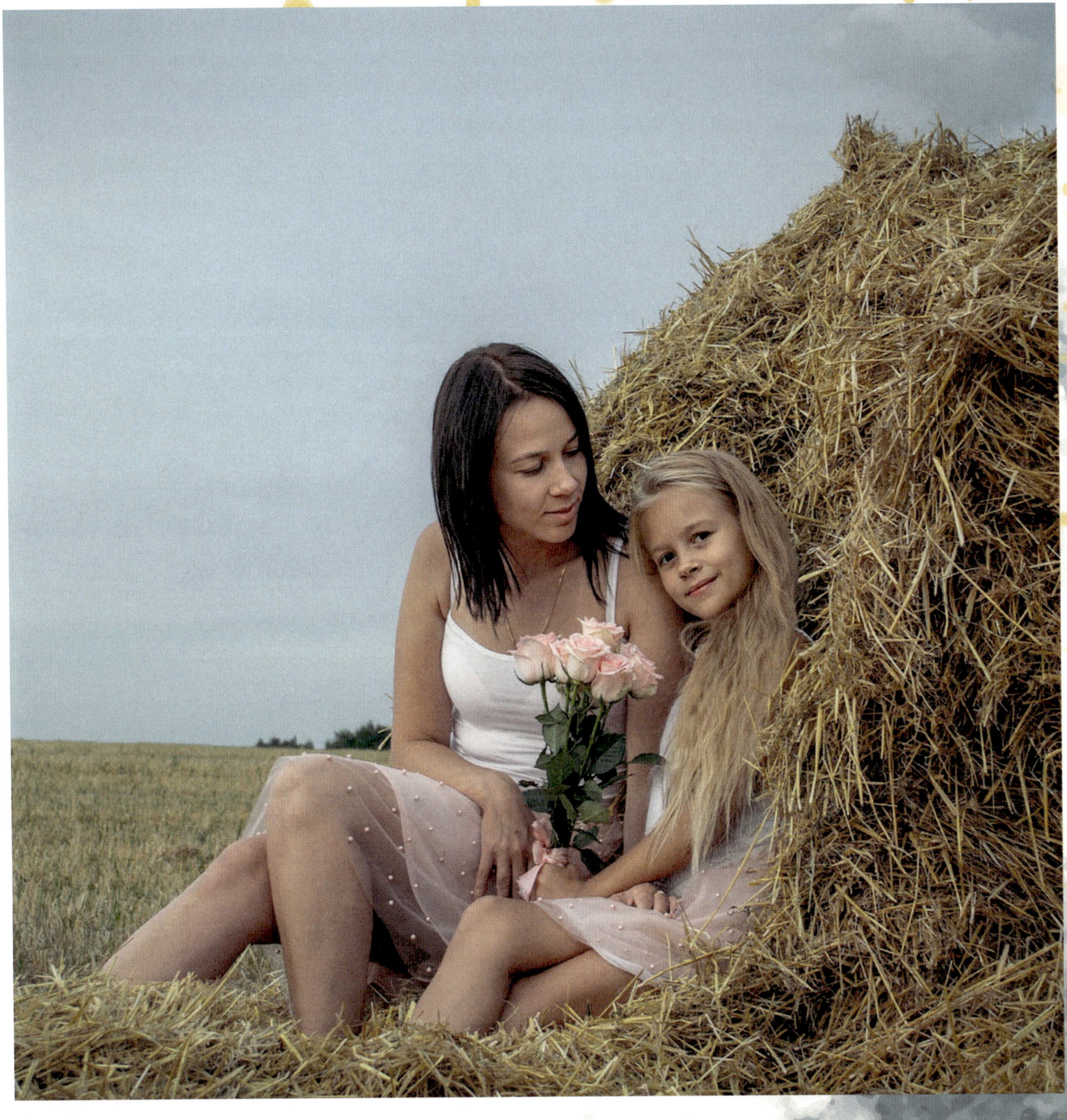

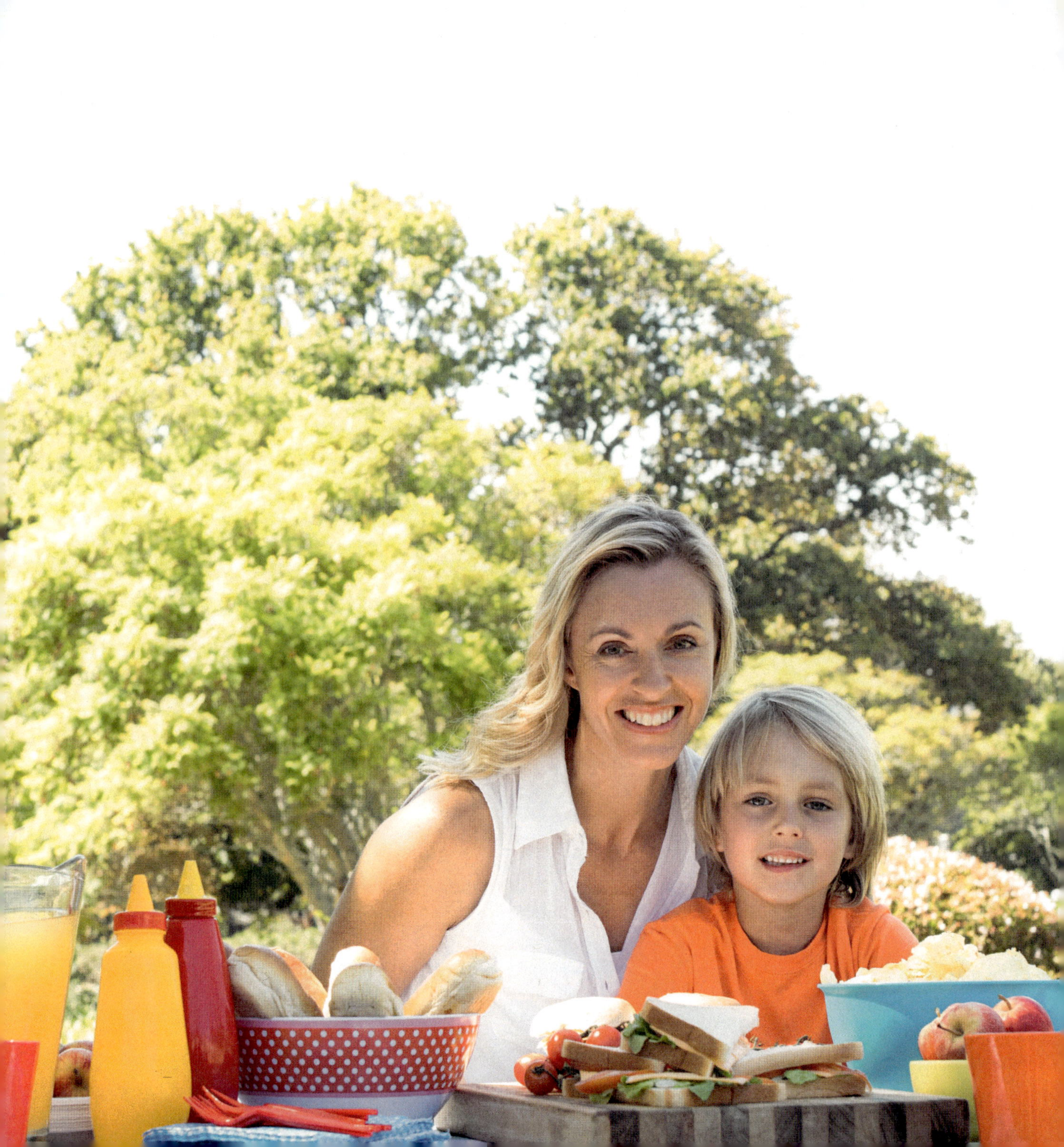

"What I love about my mum is she gives me lots of hugs and kisses. She is really cute. I love that she takes me everywhere and she makes my favourite dinner and breakfast and lunch of course."

Saxon, Age 7
Sydney, Australia

"What I love about my mum is that she gives me everything, she spoils me and I have a really good family and a good relationship."

Hudson, Age 7
Sydney, Australia

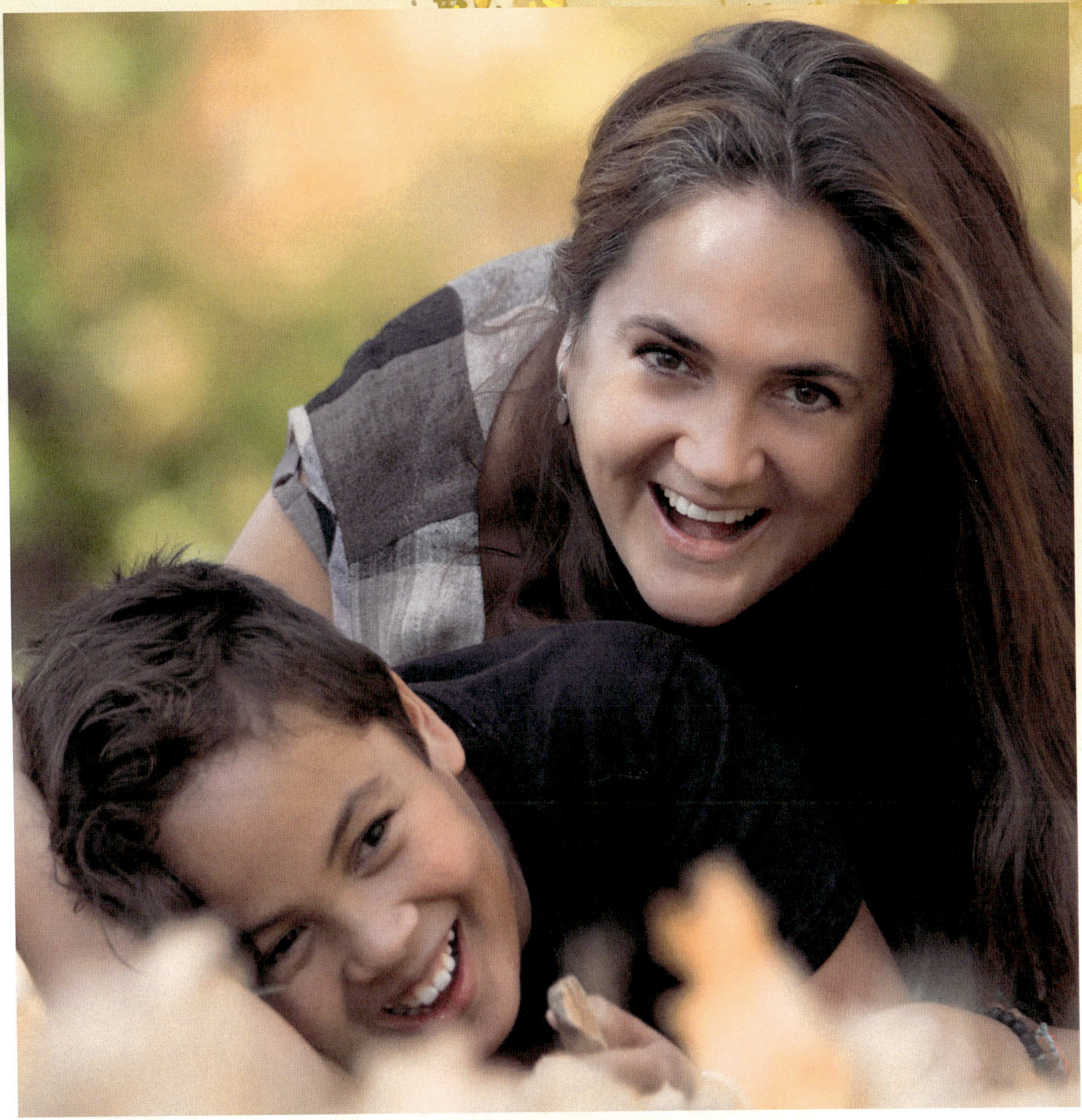

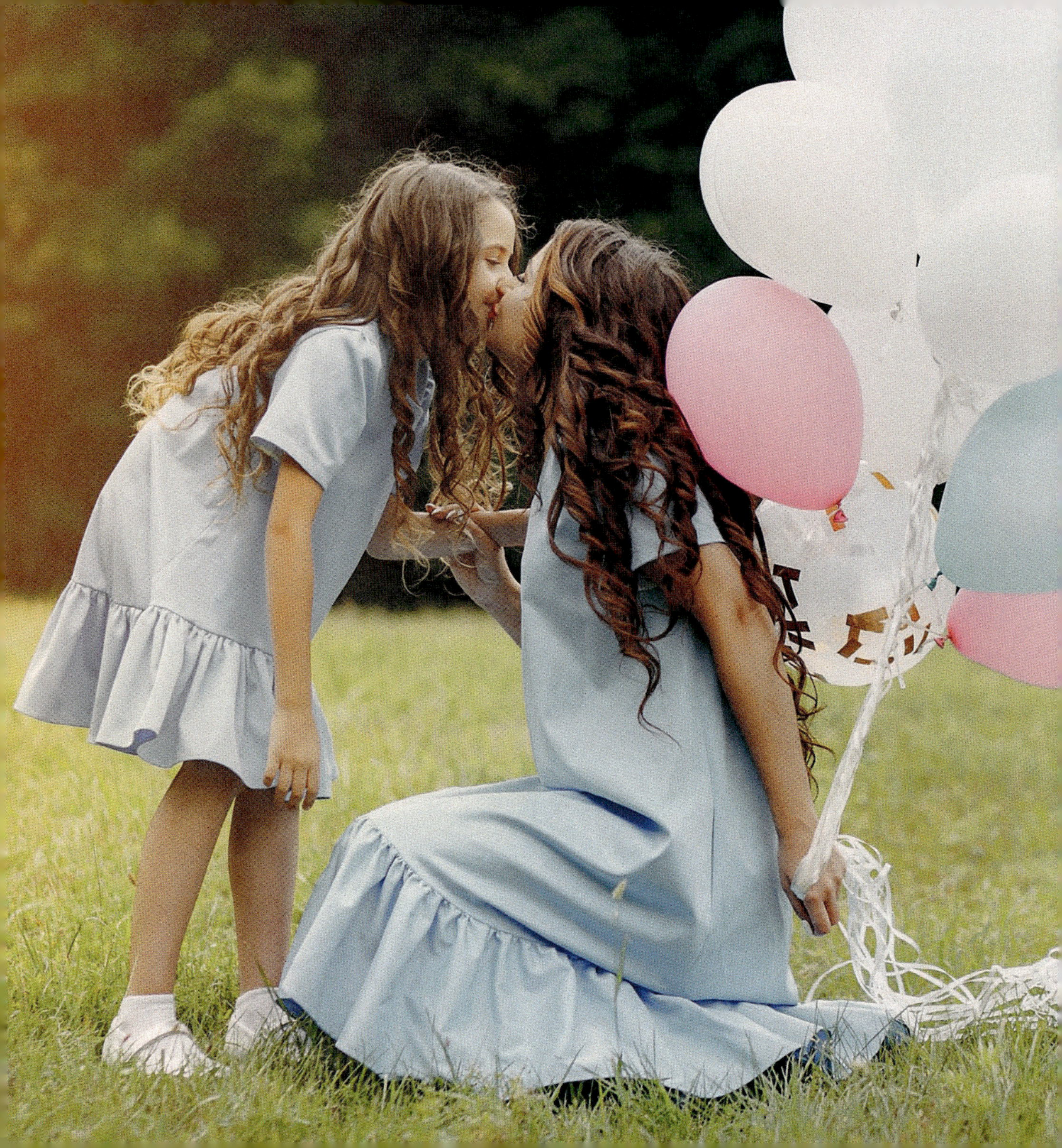

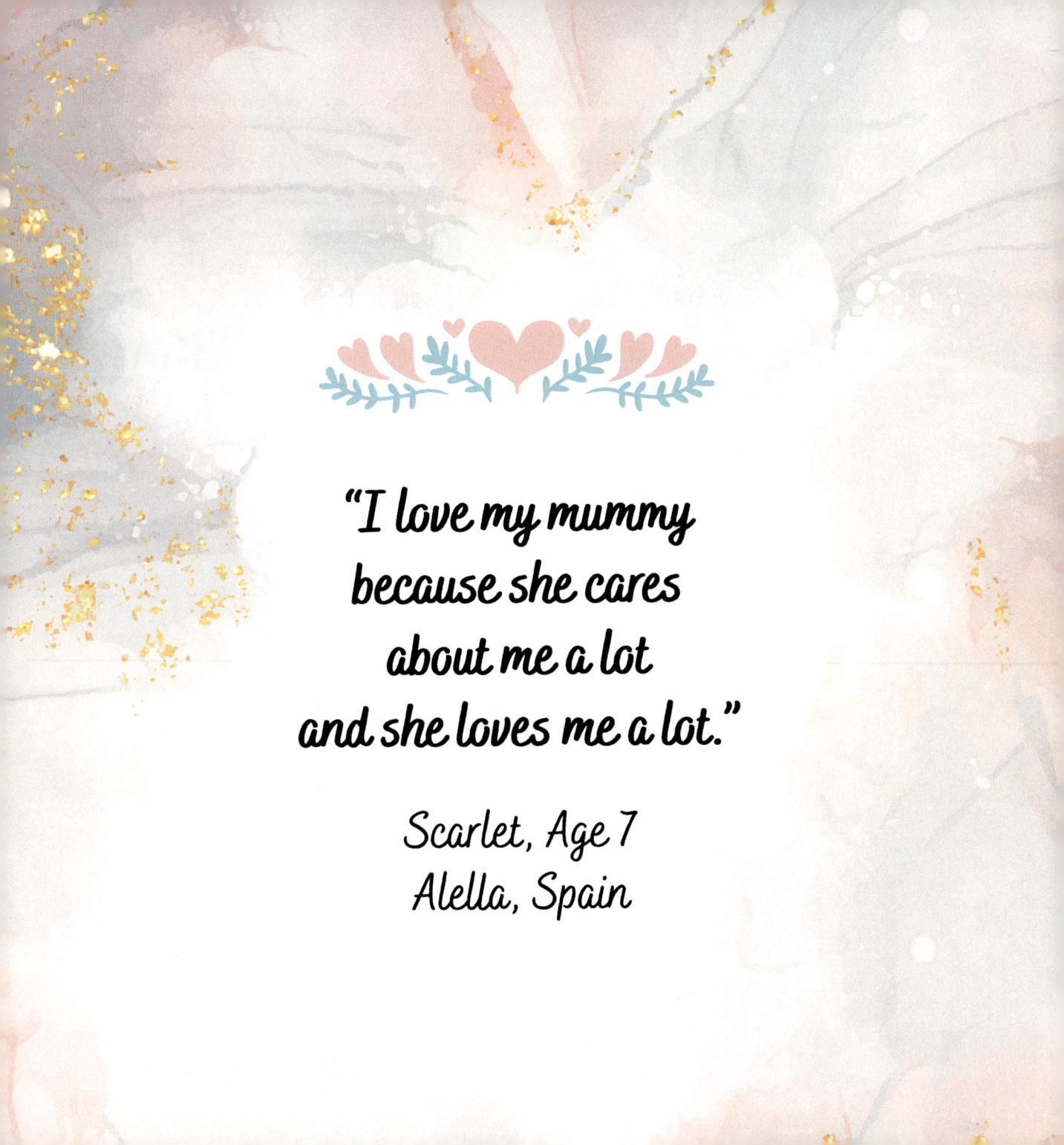

"I love my mummy
because she cares
about me a lot
and she loves me a lot."

Scarlet, Age 7
Alella, Spain

"I love mama because she bakes amazing cakes."

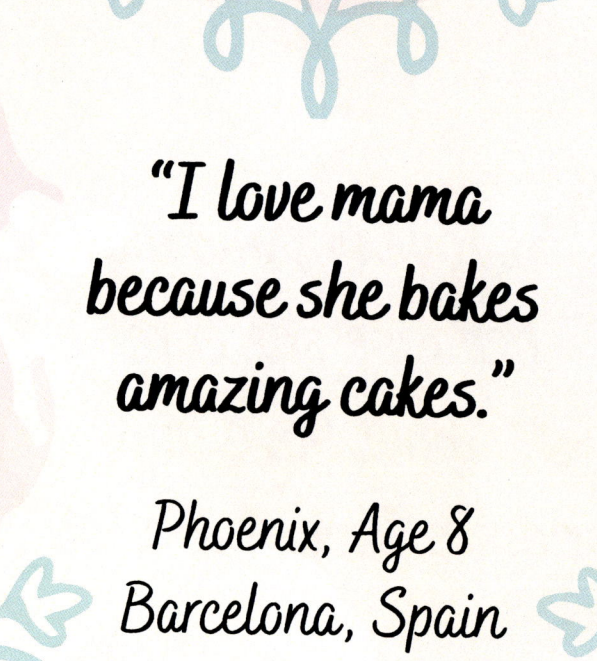

Phoenix, Age 8
Barcelona, Spain

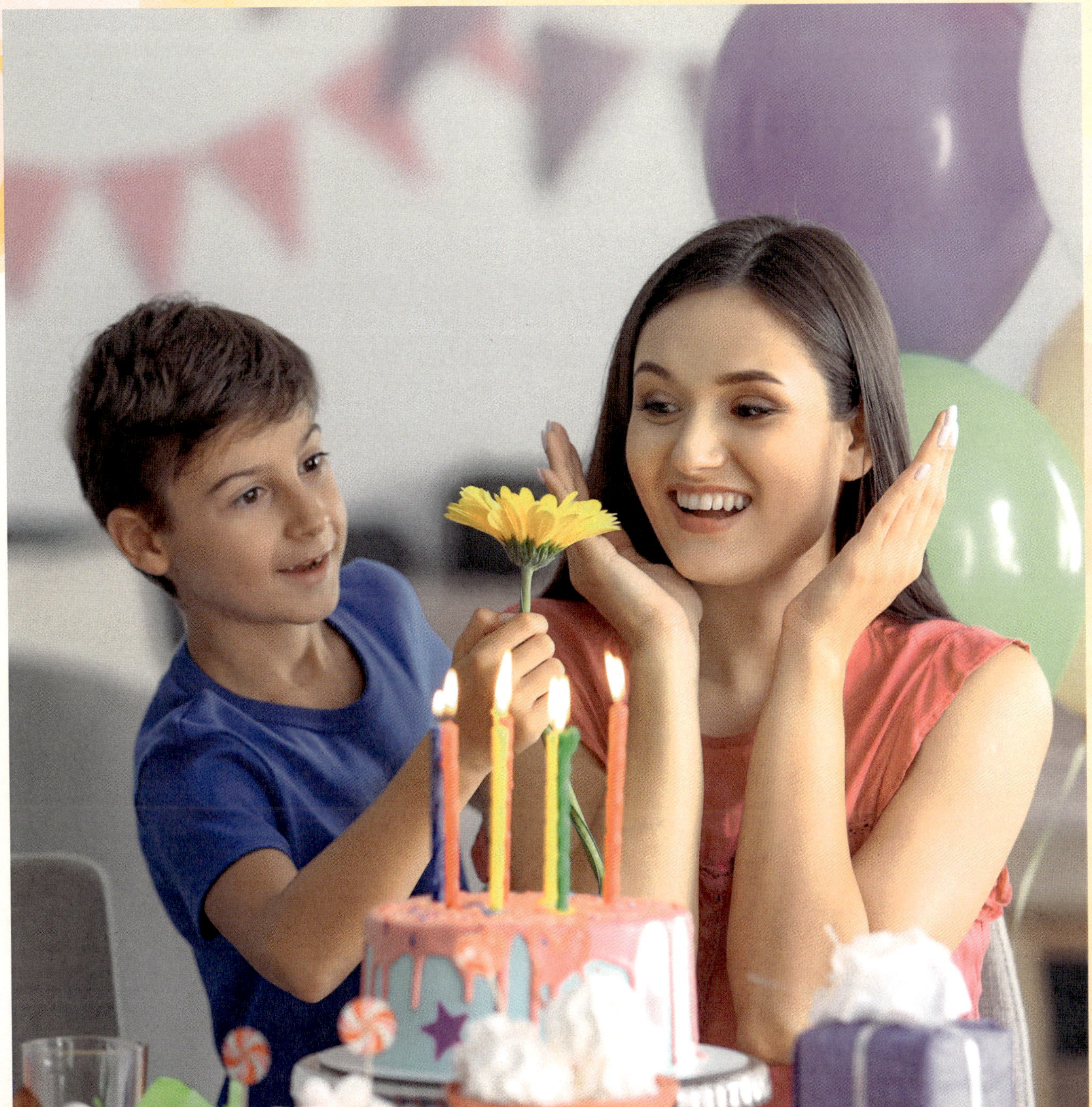

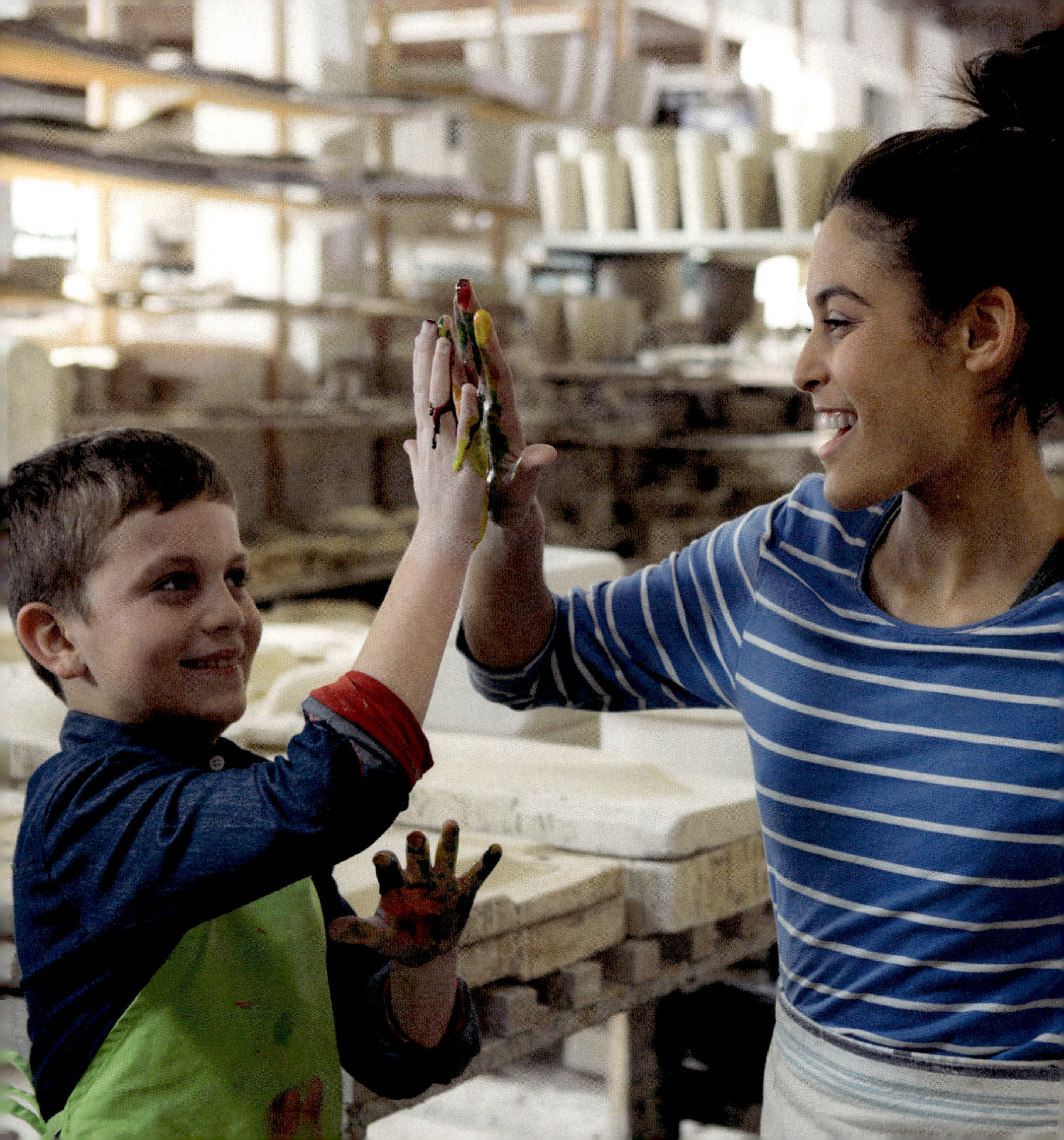

*"Mamma is loving, kind, and fun
- I love her."*

Theodore, Age 8
Sydney, Australia

"I love that my mom takes care of me. She bakes magnificent cakes."

Sula, Age 8
Barcelona, Spain

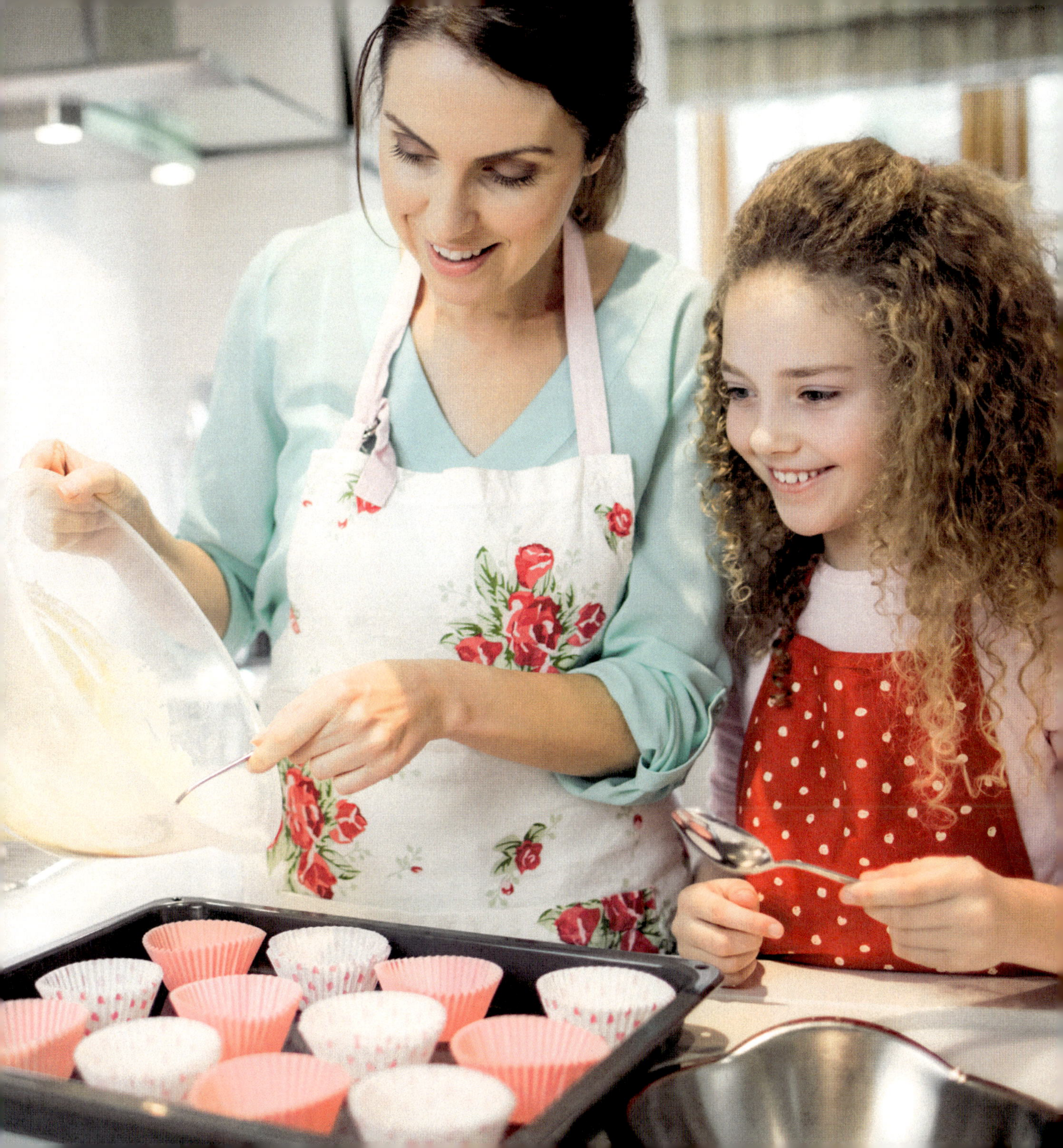

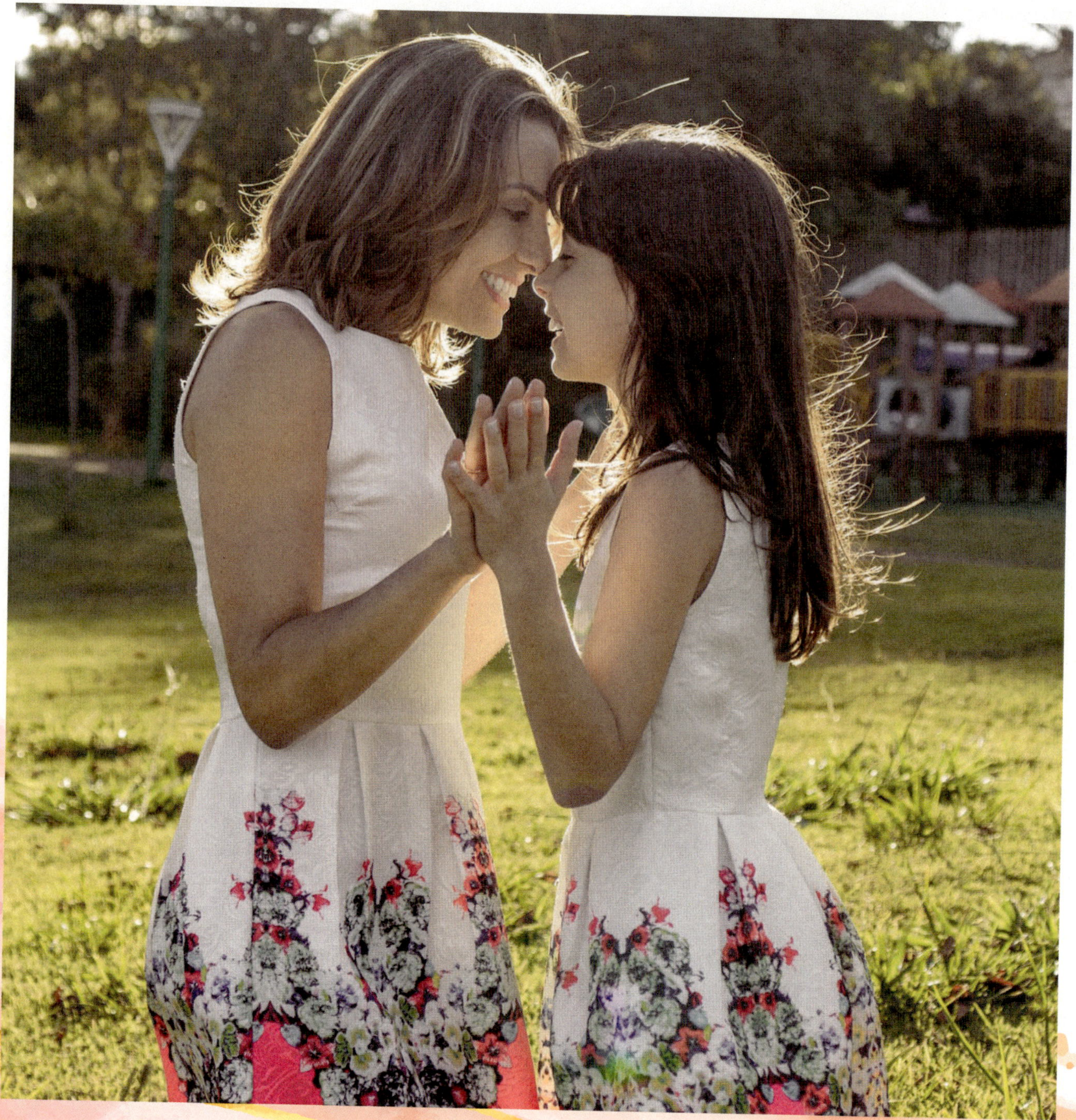

"What I love about my mommy
is she takes care of us,
that she is responsible,
and she knows what to do,
and she's nice."

Sophie, Age 8
Paris, France

"I love about my mom
how her eyes shine
when she looks at me and
all she does for me and my brother."

Leon, Age 9
Zagreb, Croatia

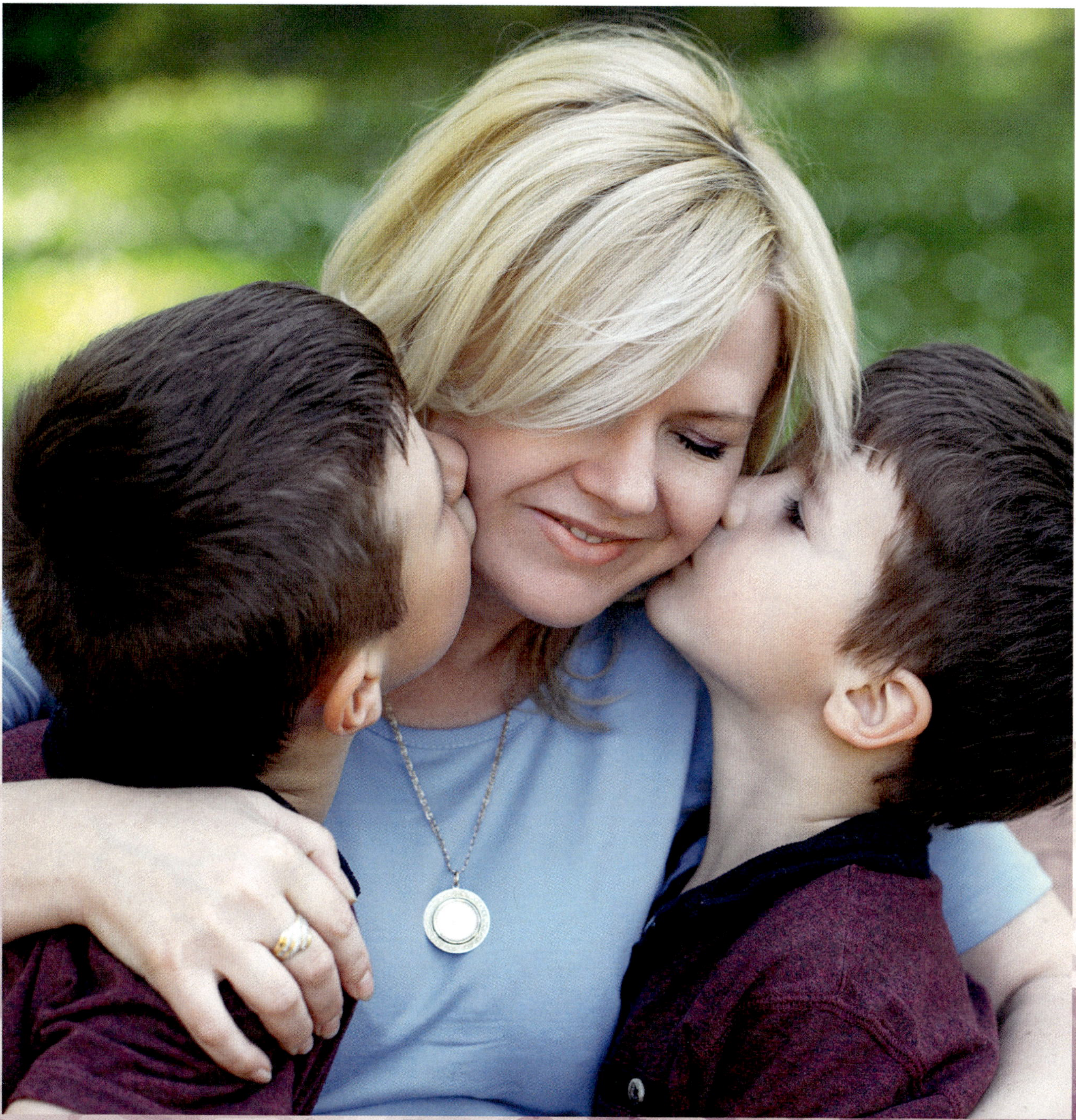

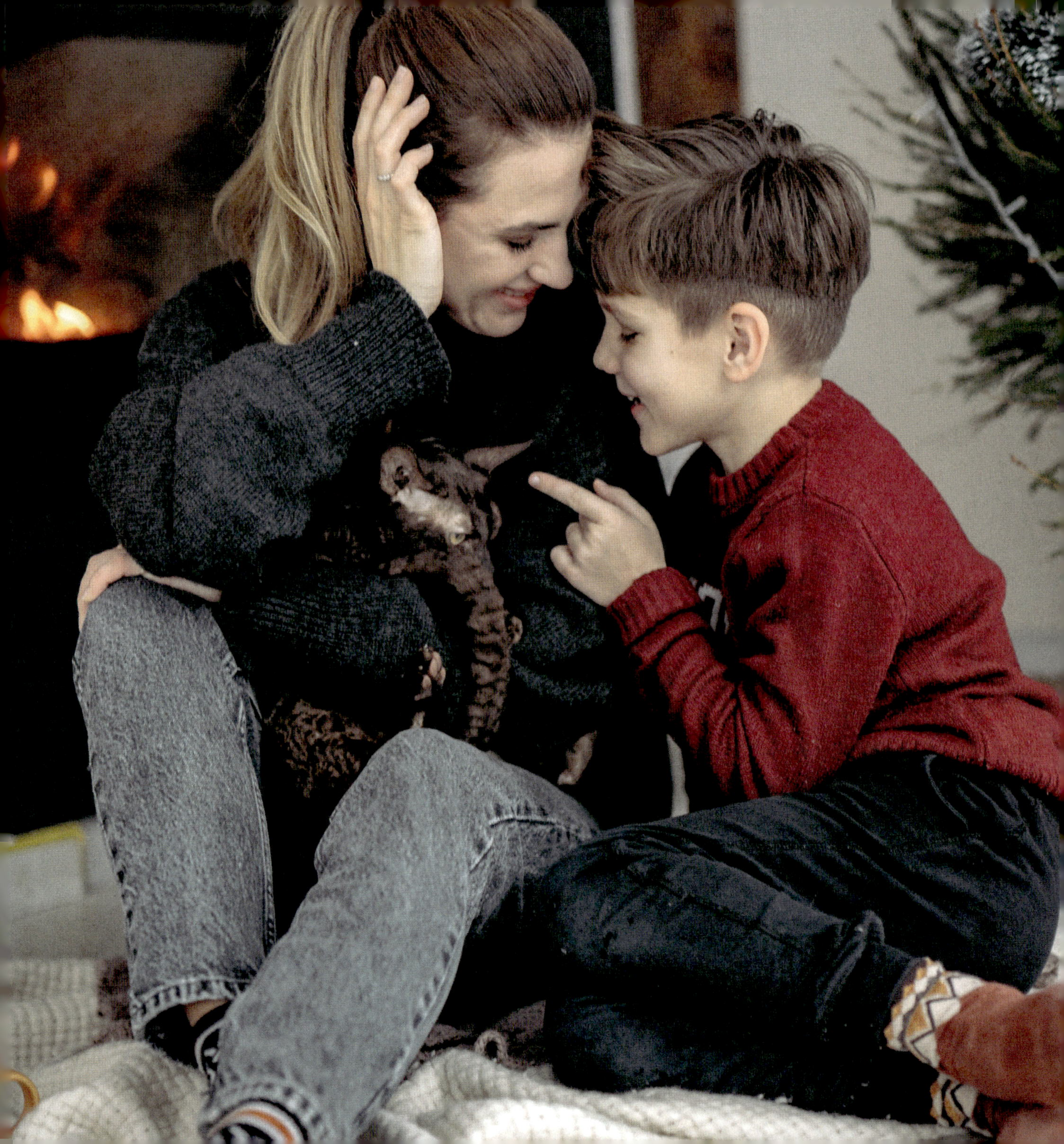

"What I love about my mum is she likes cats and makes me bubble tea."

Curtis, Age 9
Sydney, Australia

"I love my mummy because she always makes me laugh when I'm feeling sad."

*Raphael, Age 10
Barcelona, Spain*

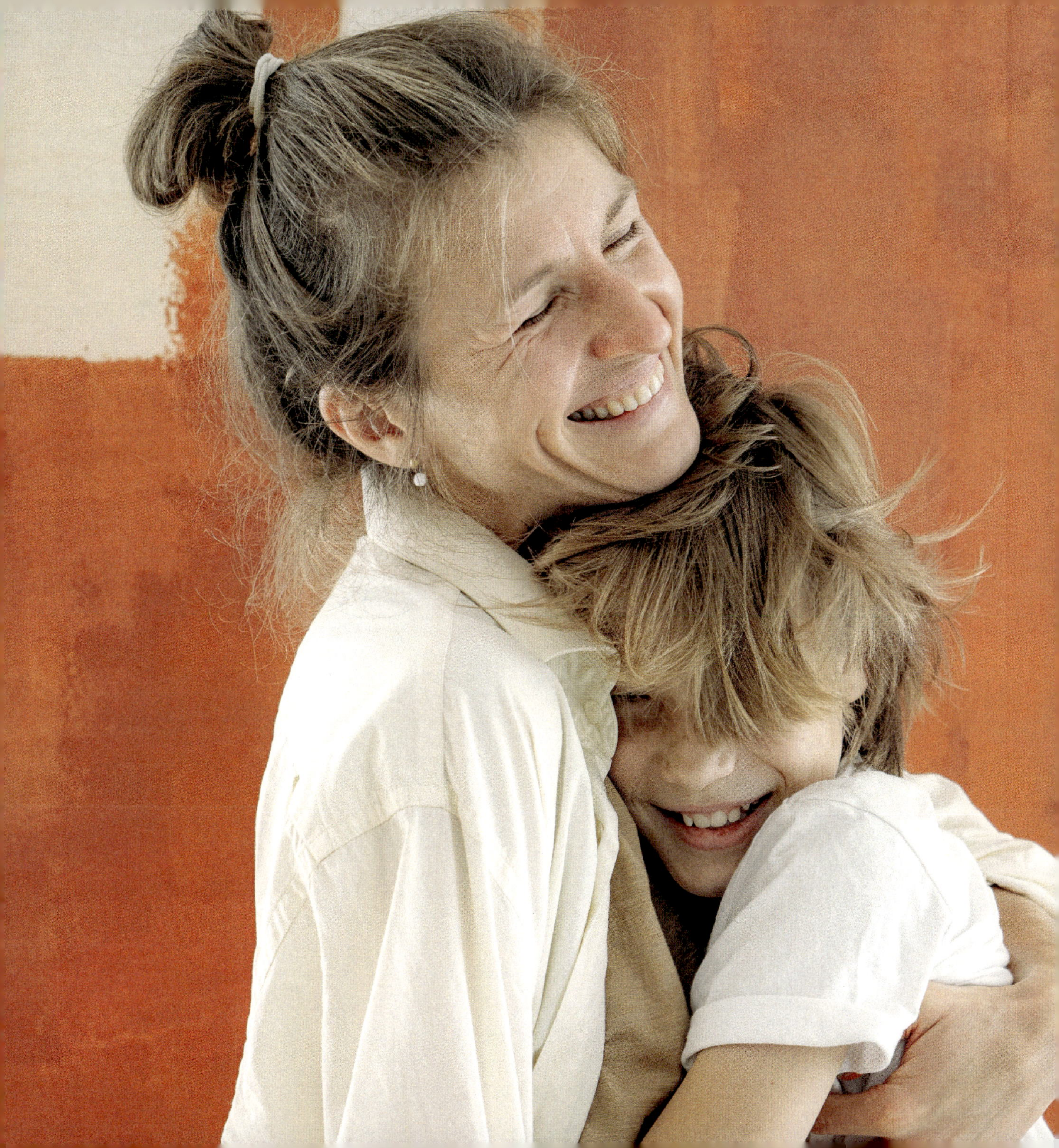

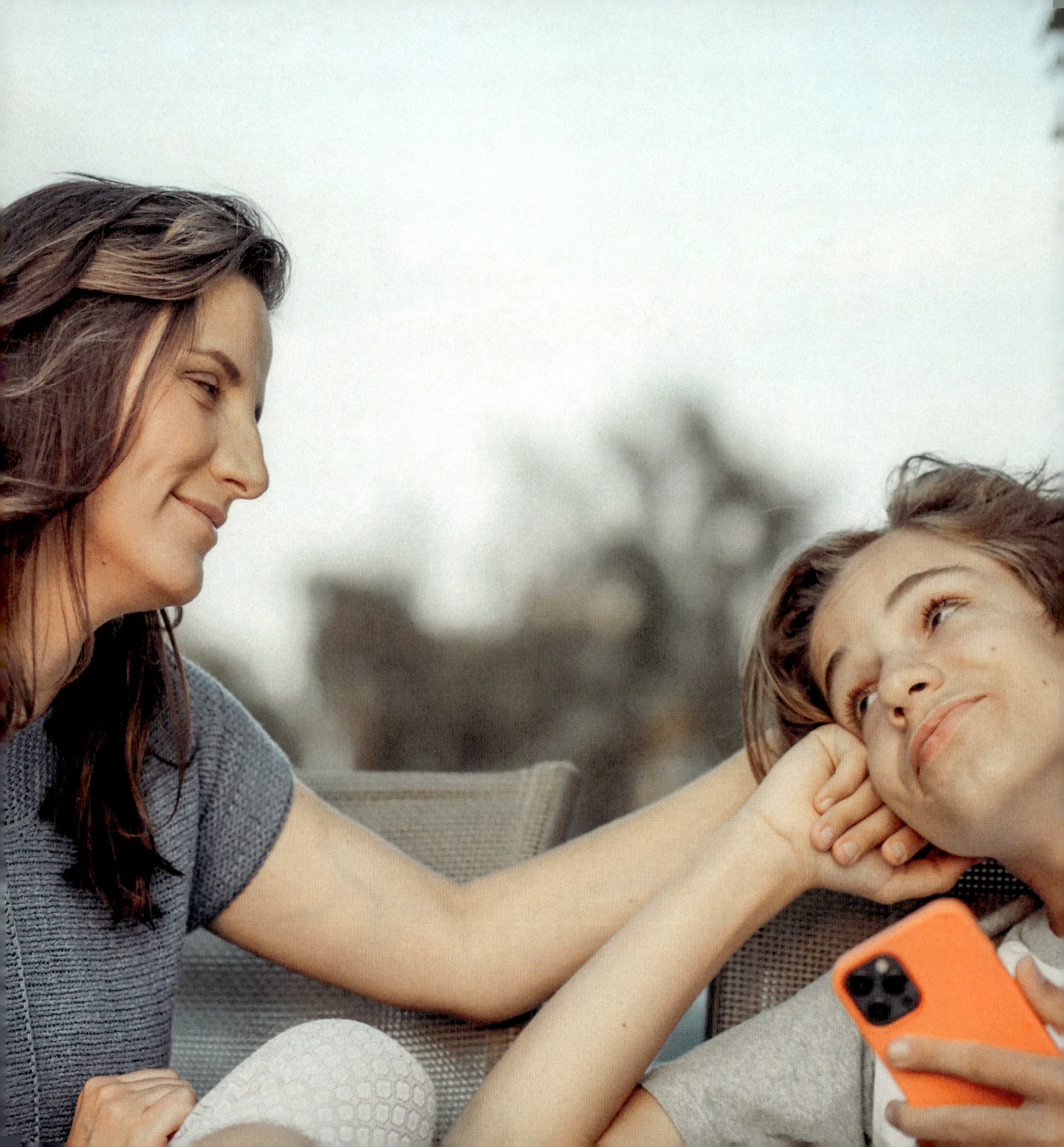

"What I love most about my mom is that she's a very good mom, she is always there for me and that she is always generous."

David, Age 11
Johannesburg, South Africa

"I love my mum more than the moon and more than the planets. I just love her and can't find the words to express it."

Harrison, Age 11
Oxford, United Kingdom

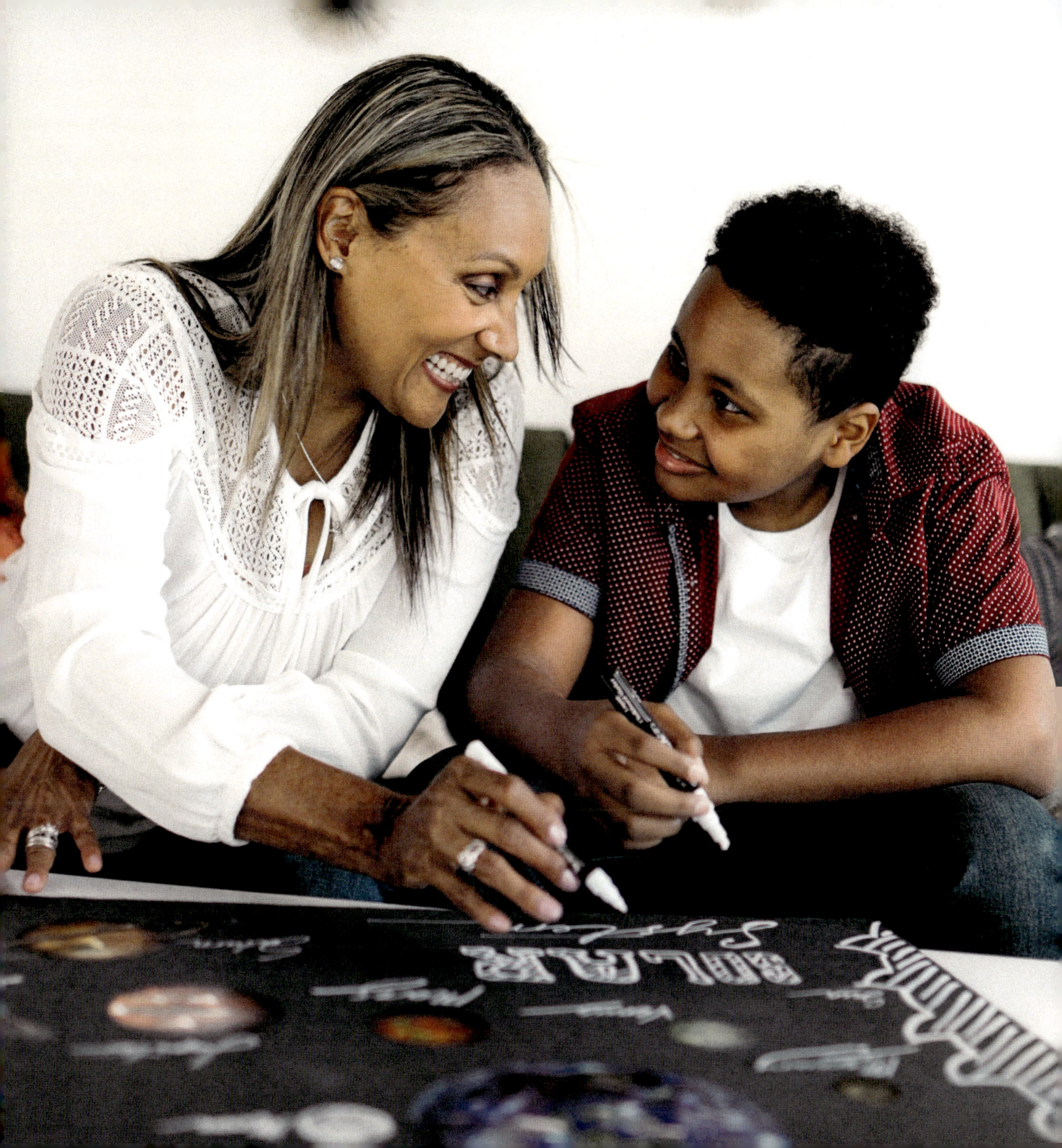

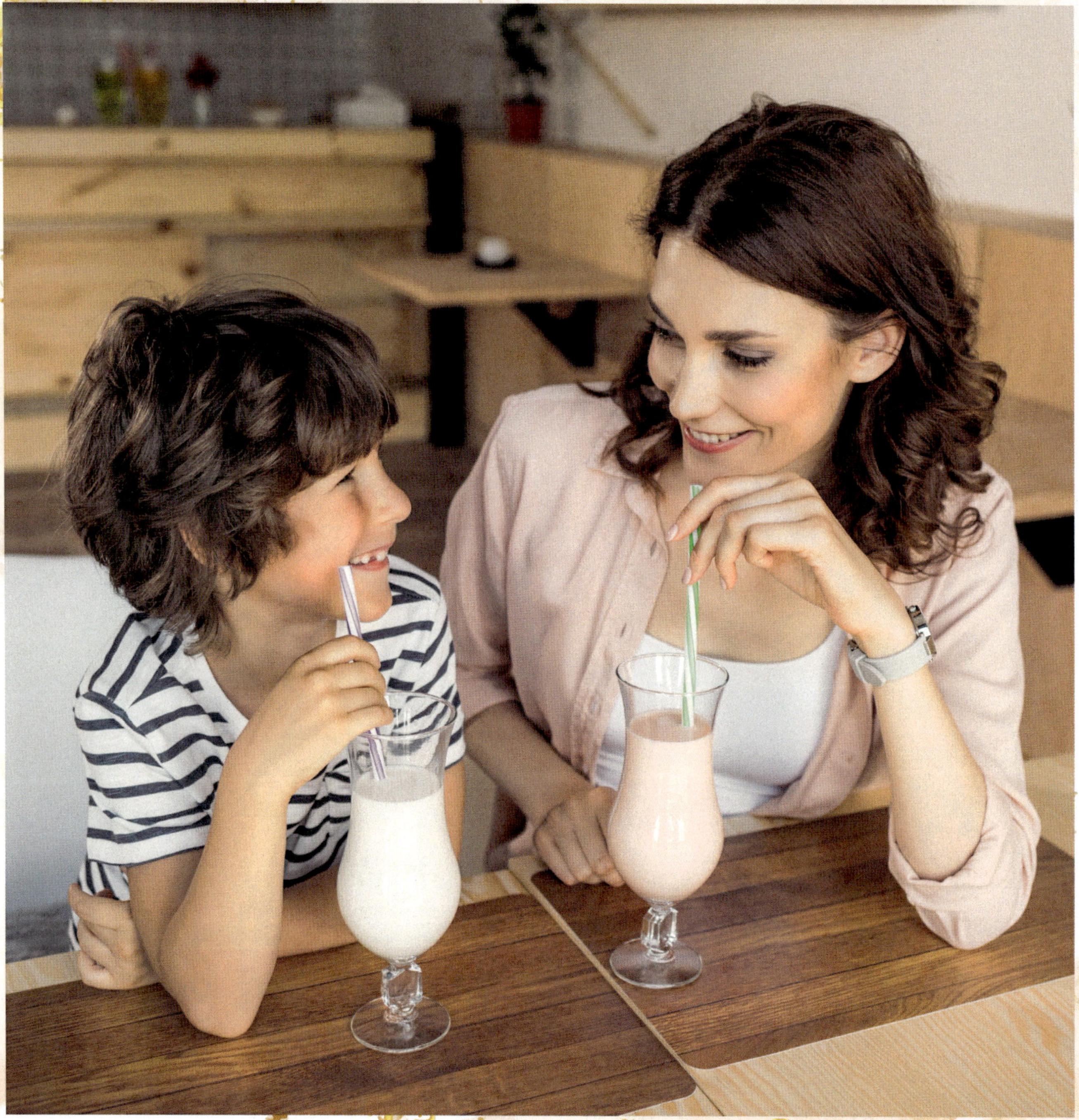

"What I love about my mum is she is nice and gives me hugs. She makes me delicious drinks like chocolate milkshakes and passion fruit sodas with ice cream."

Erik, Age 11
Sydney, Australia

"I love my mom because she loves me and because she comforts me when I am sad."

Lukas, Age 11
Zagreb, Croatia

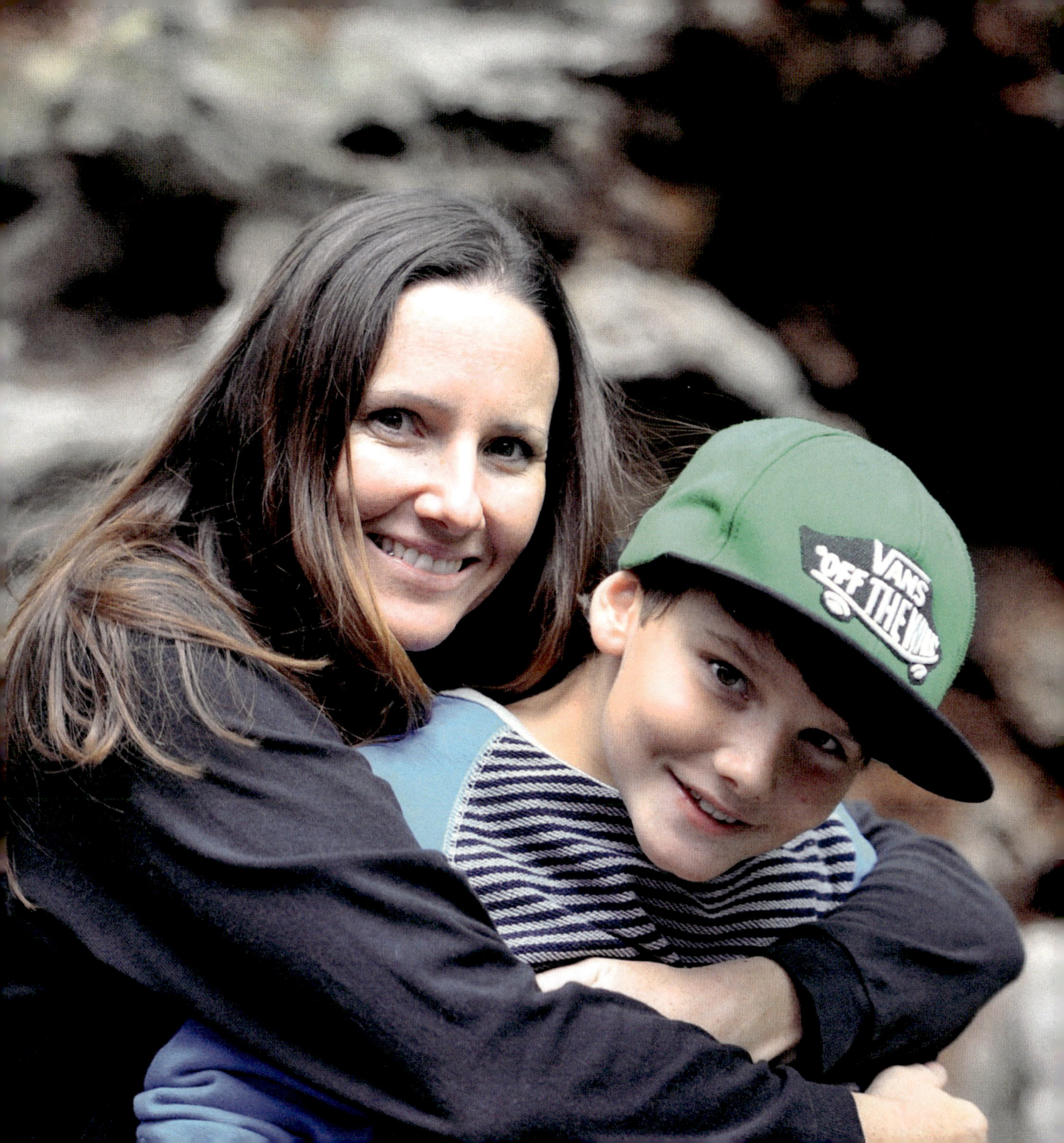
VANS
"OFF THE WALL"

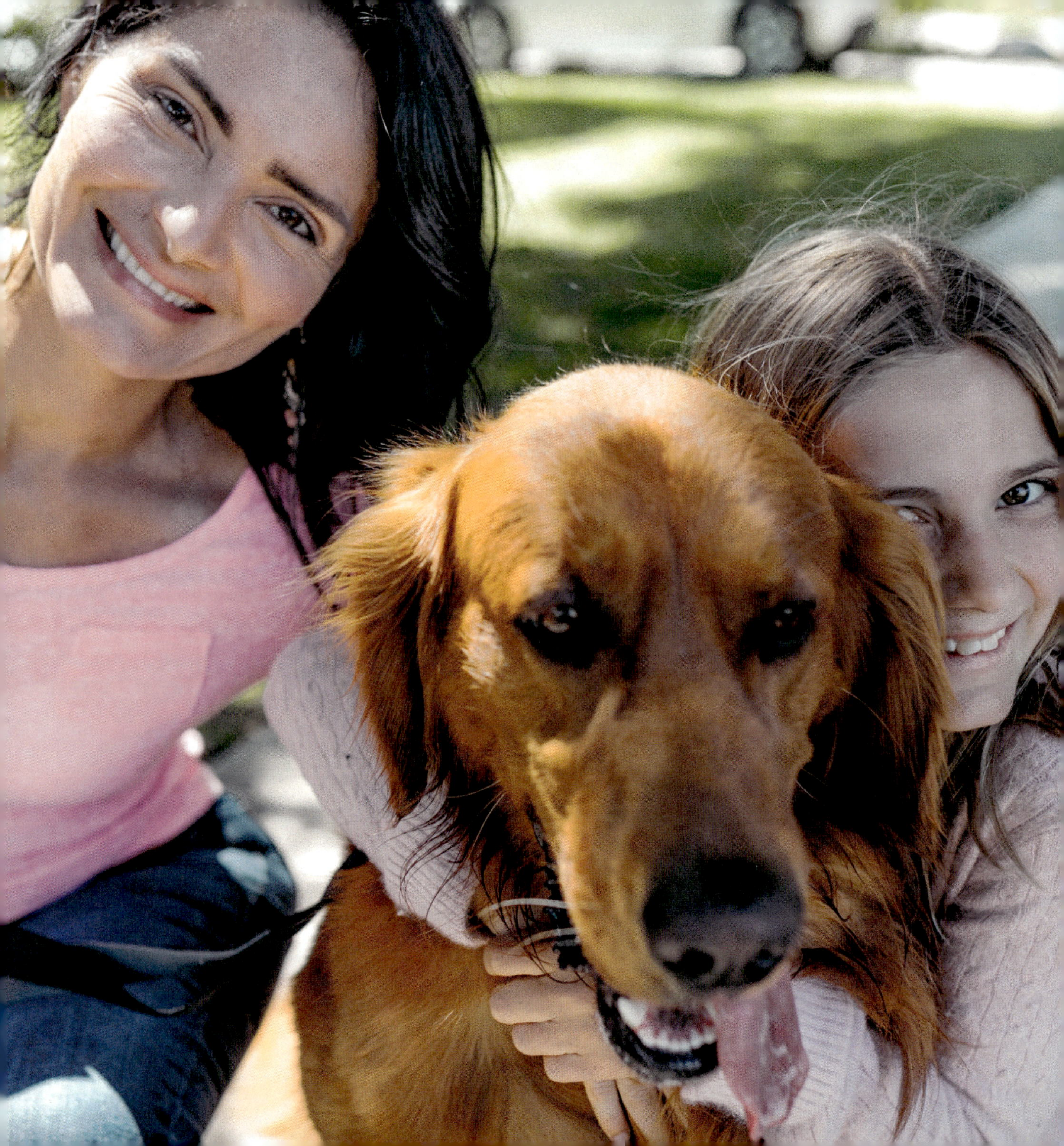

"I am so beyond grateful to have my Mumma in my life as my mum and my friend. I love talking with her, laughing with her, crying with her, and yelling with her to try and let the dog go on my bed."

Clementine, Age 11
Sydney, Australia

"I love my mom because she teaches us how to cook and bake and is very kind."

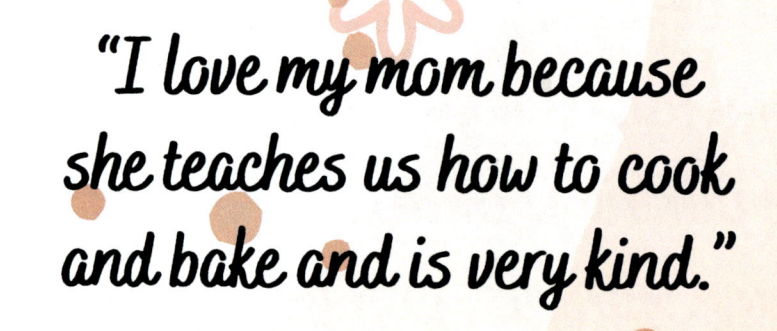

Isabella, Age 12
Cape Town, South Africa

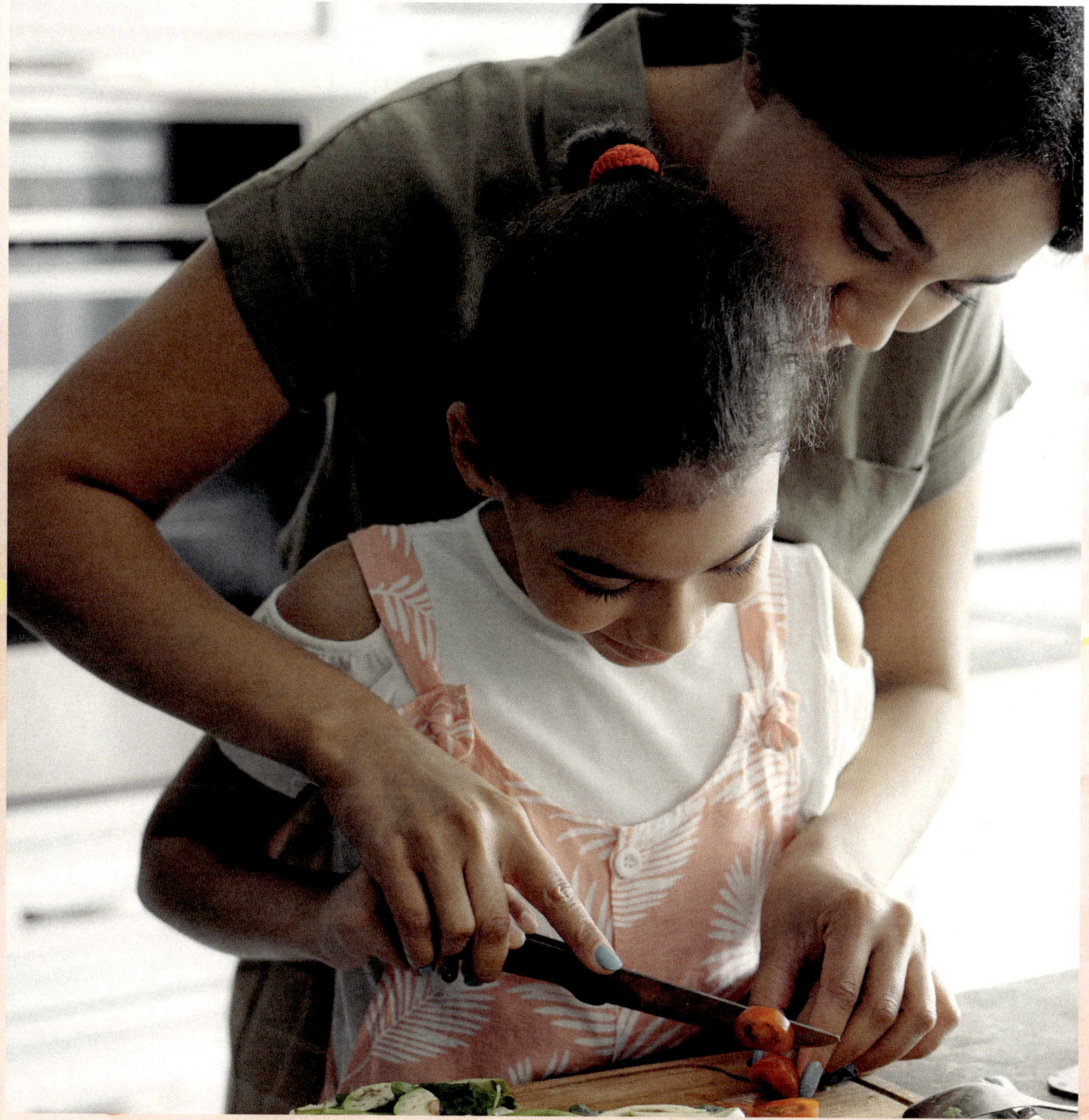

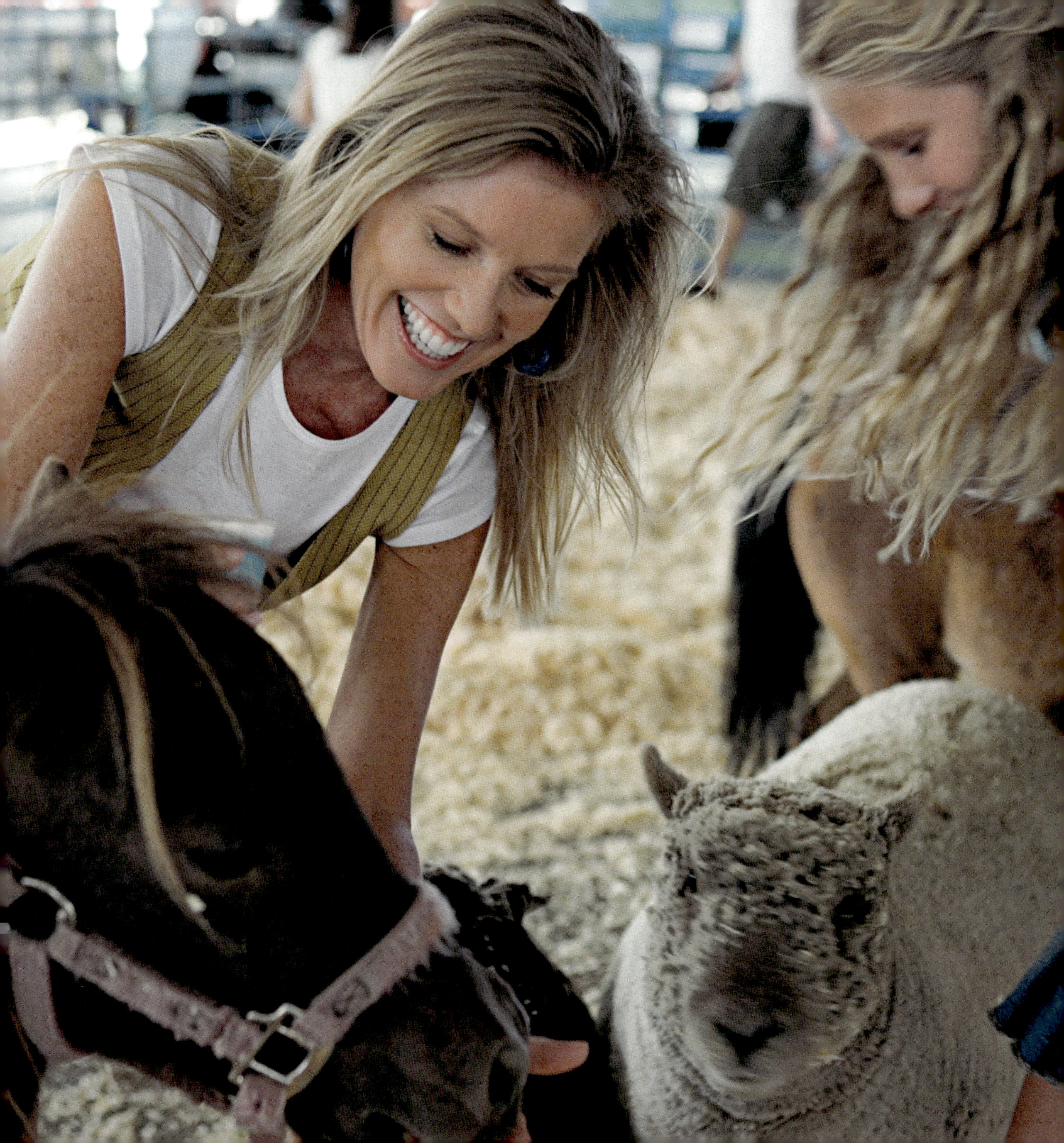

"What I love most about my mom
is she tries her hardest
to give us what we want or need,
she loves animals, she loves me a lot,
and is always there for me."

Caidee-Ann, Age 12
Johannesburg, South Africa

"When I hang out with my mom for hours, it feel like seconds. When my mom yells at me, I know she cares for me. When my mom feeds me, I know she wants me to grow. Best of all, when my mom says, 'I love you,' she means it."

Sophia, Age 12
Fountain Valley, California

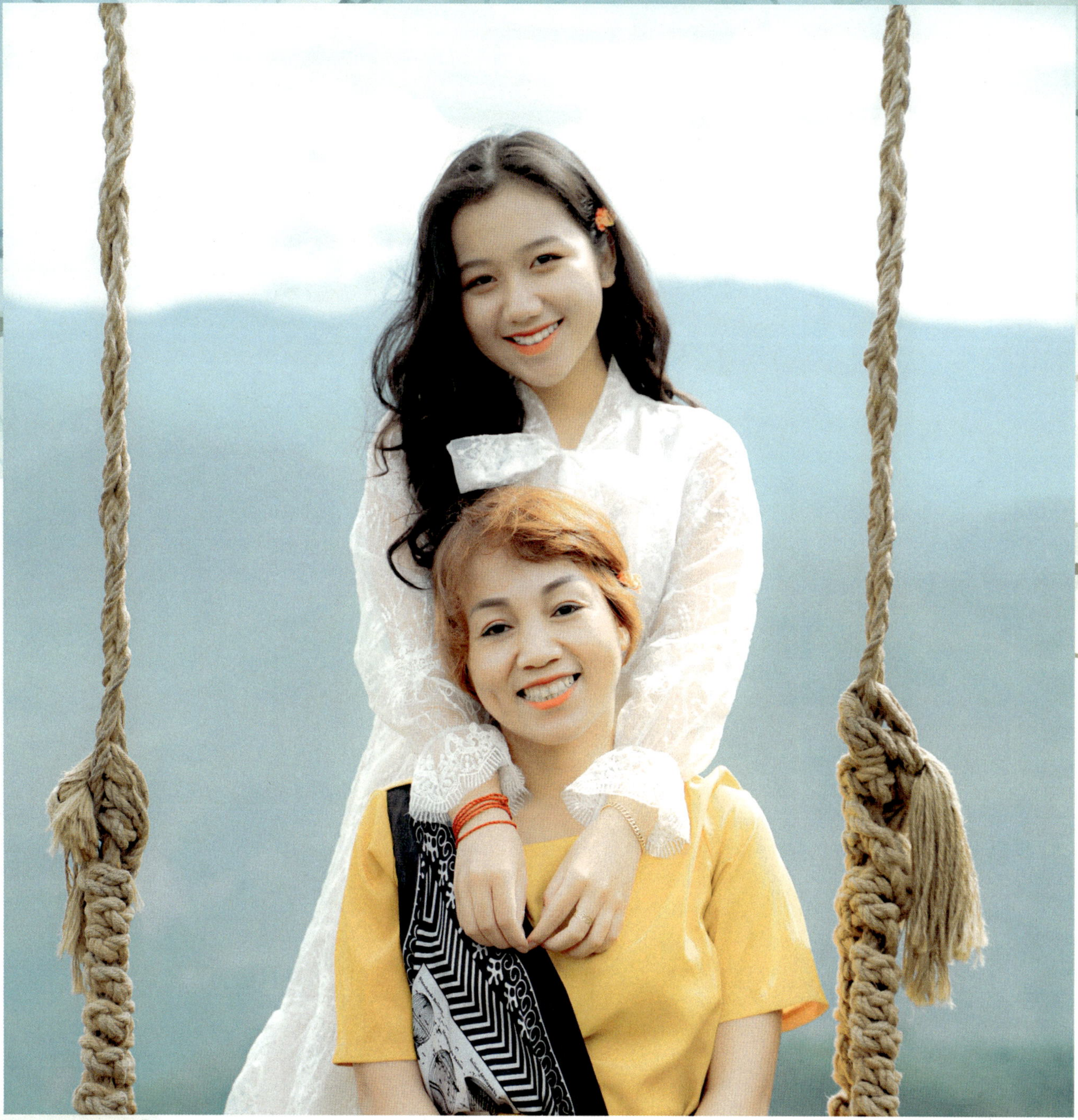

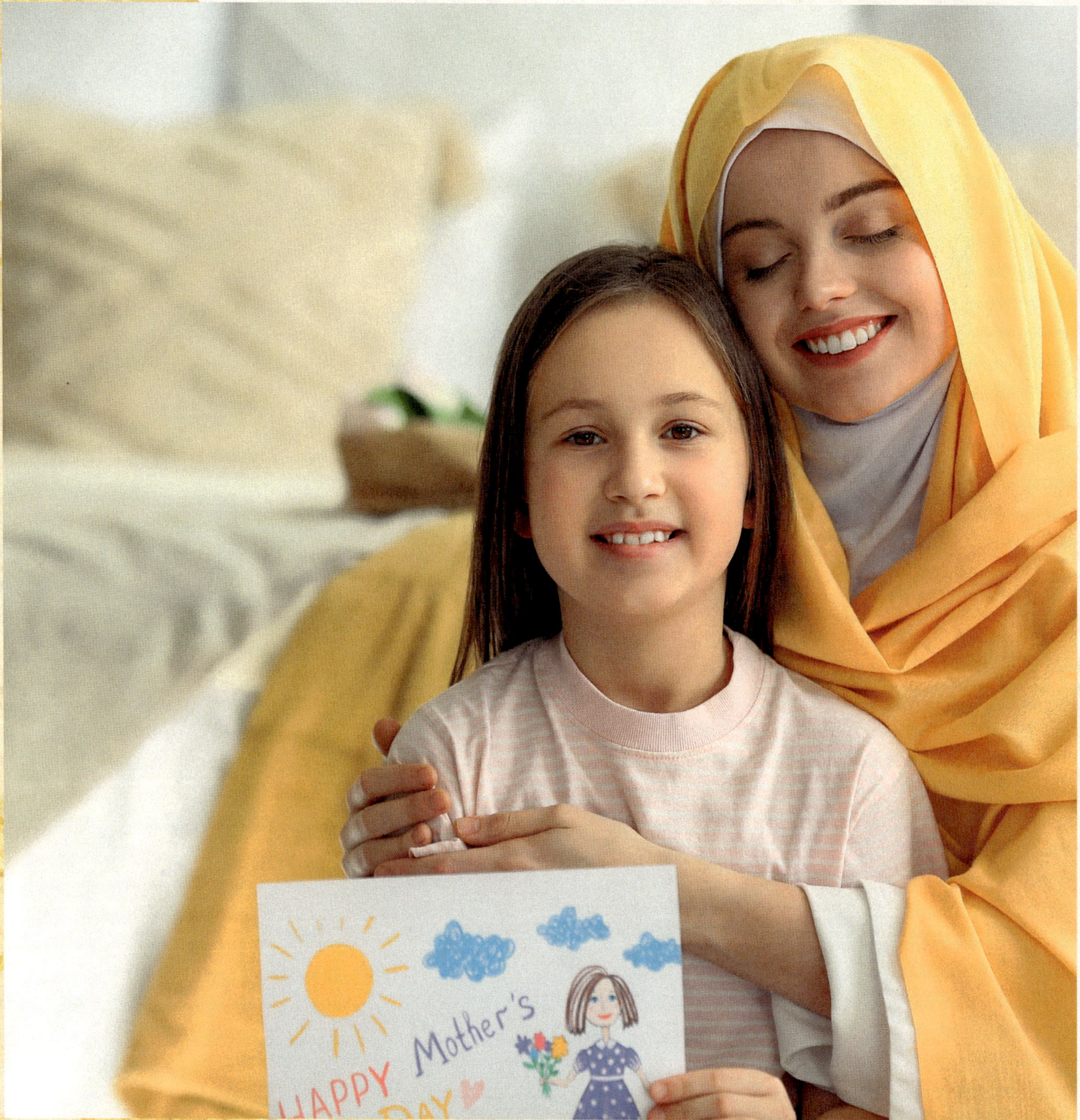
HAPPY Mother's
DAY

"I love my mom because she is loving, kind, and teaches us about a world of endless possibilities."

Gabriella, Age 12
Cape Town, South Africa

"I love that my mom is caring and is a good listener."

Alayna, Age 13
Orange County, California

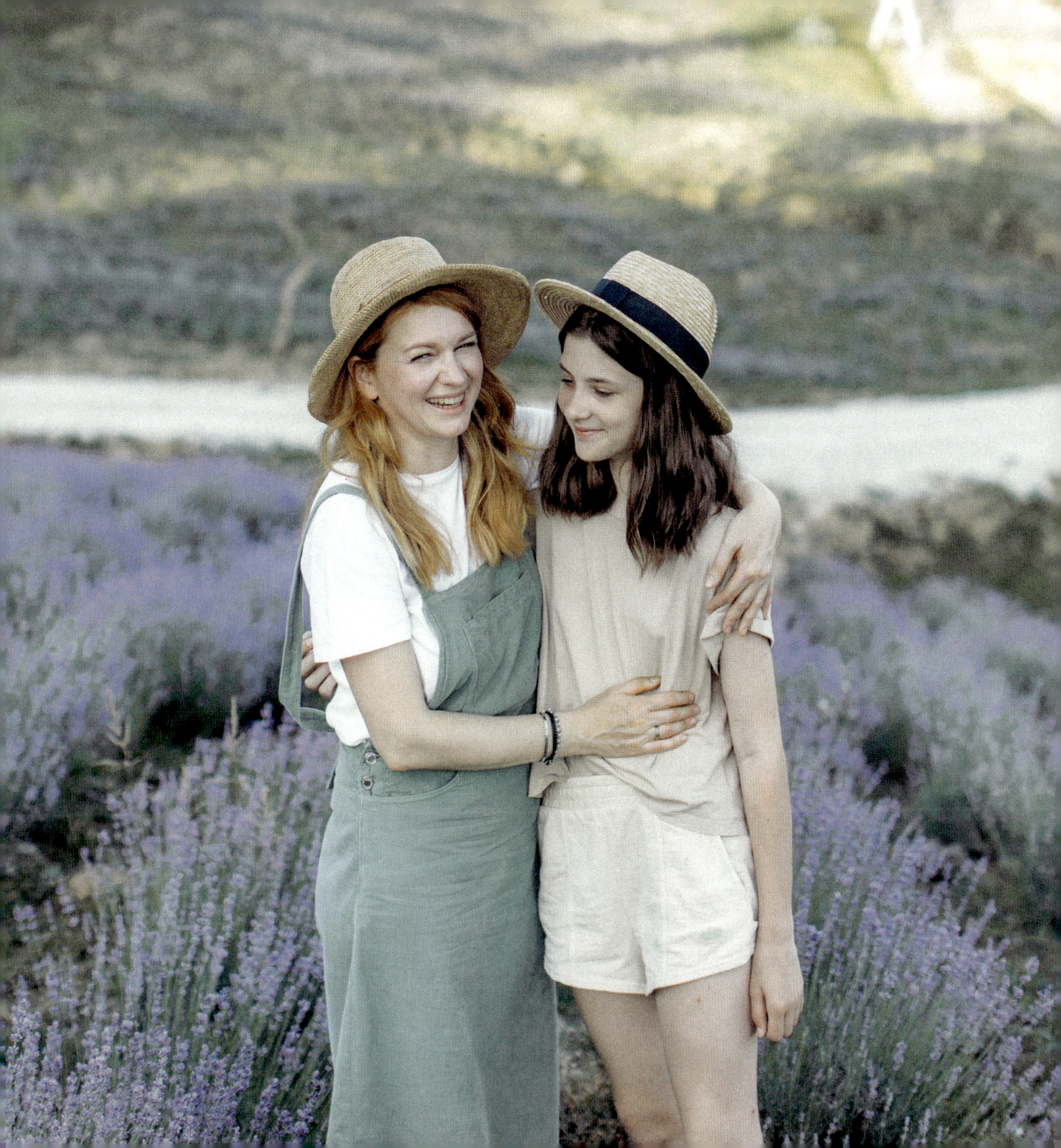

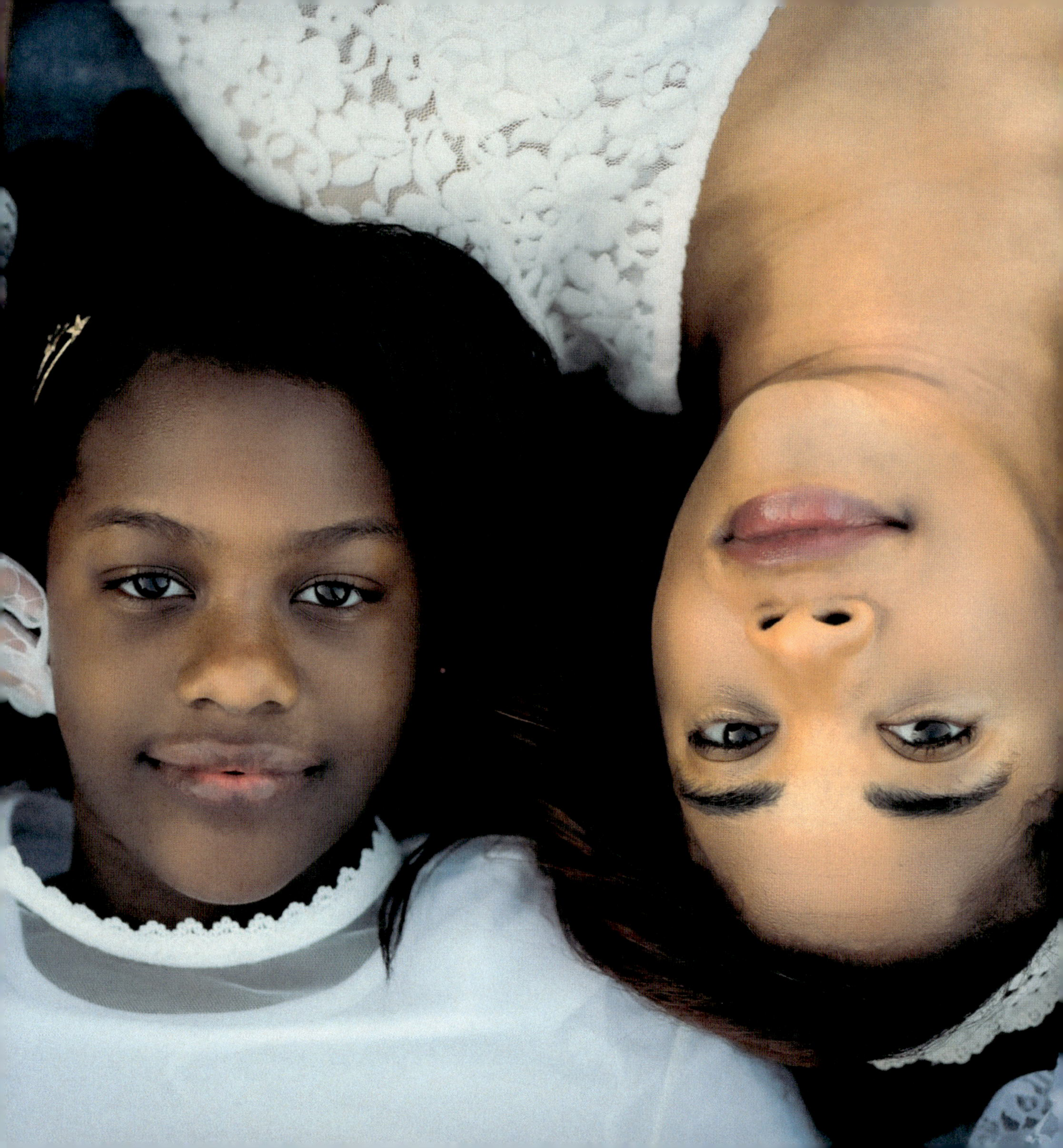

"What I love about
my meme is she's caring
and gives good advice."

Kadynce, Age 13
Atlanta, Georgia

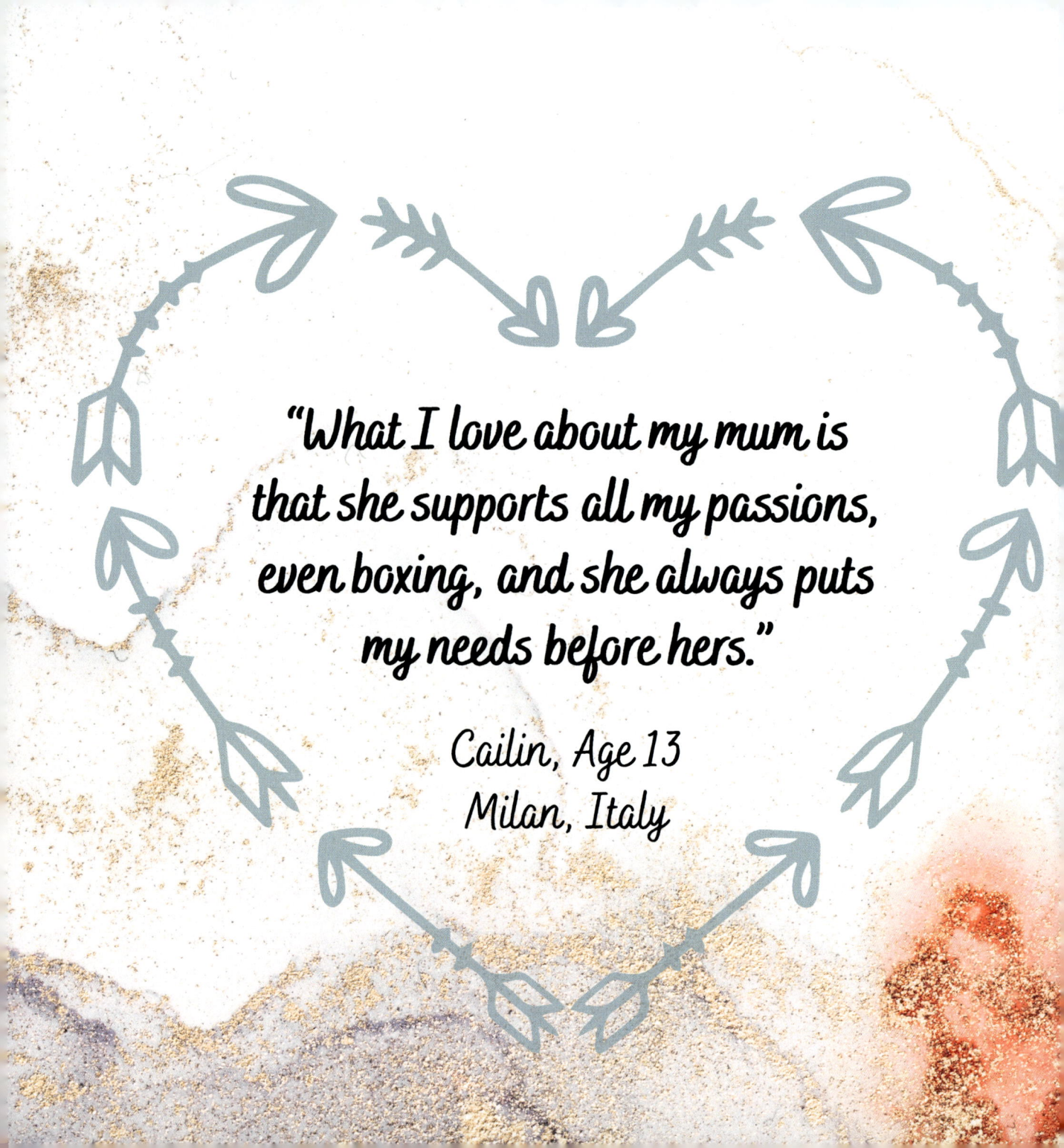

"What I love about my mum is that she supports all my passions, even boxing, and she always puts my needs before hers."

Cailin, Age 13
Milan, Italy

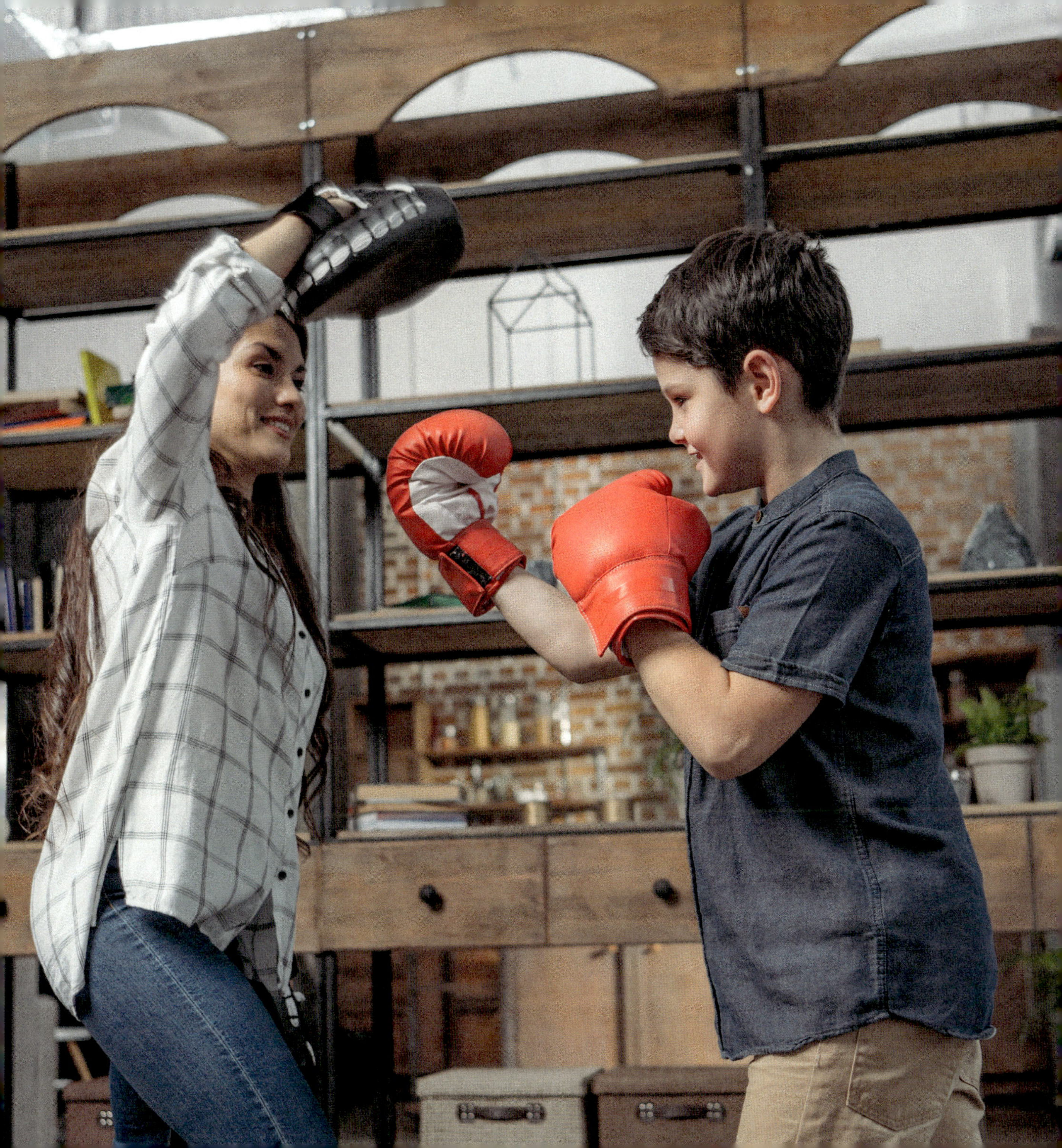

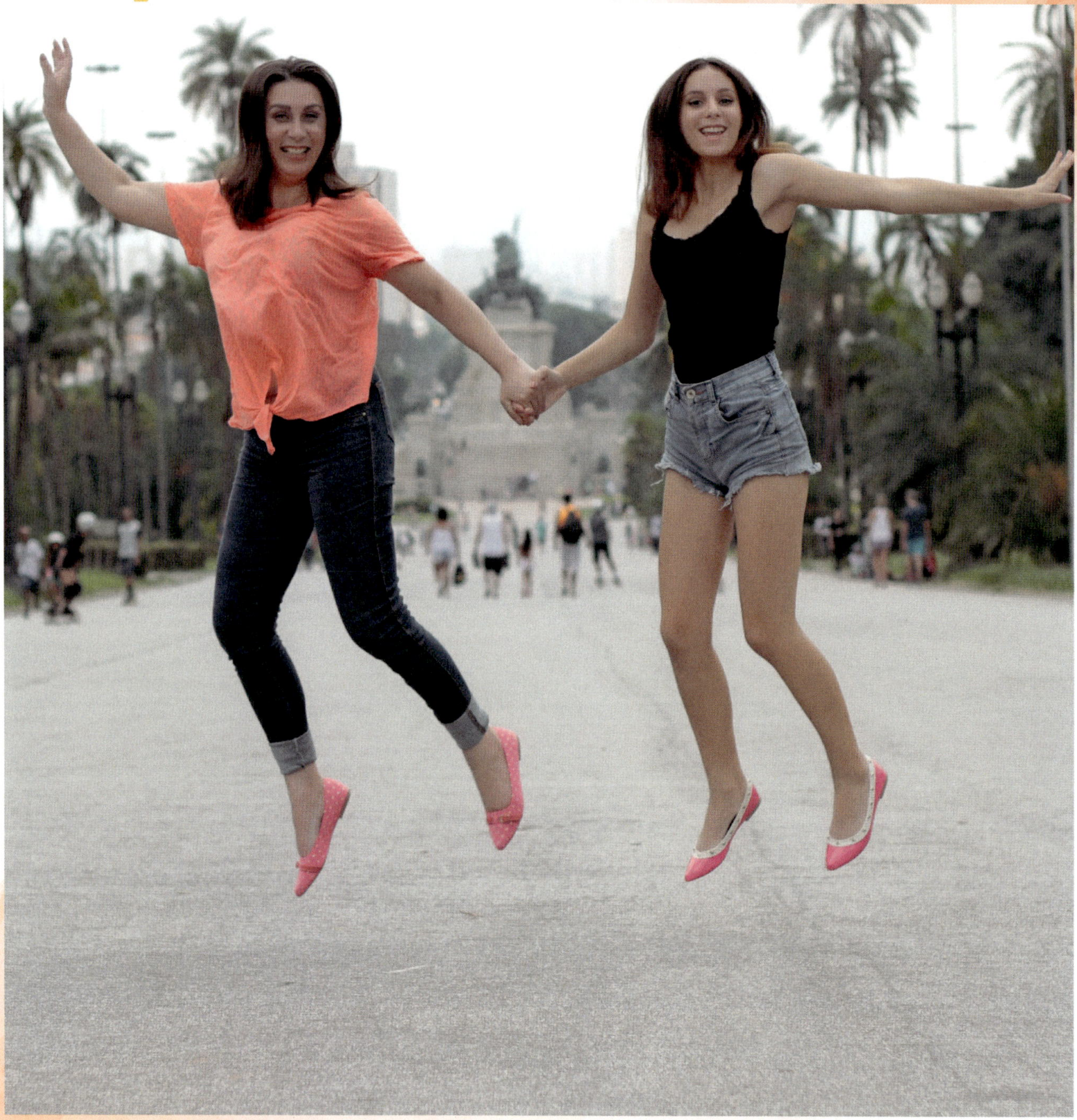

*"Moral support
is what my mom gives best.
I am not me without my mom's wings."*

Megan, Age 13
Fountain Valley, California

*"What I love
about my mom is
that she is very gracious."*

Sophie, Age 15
Bakersfield, California

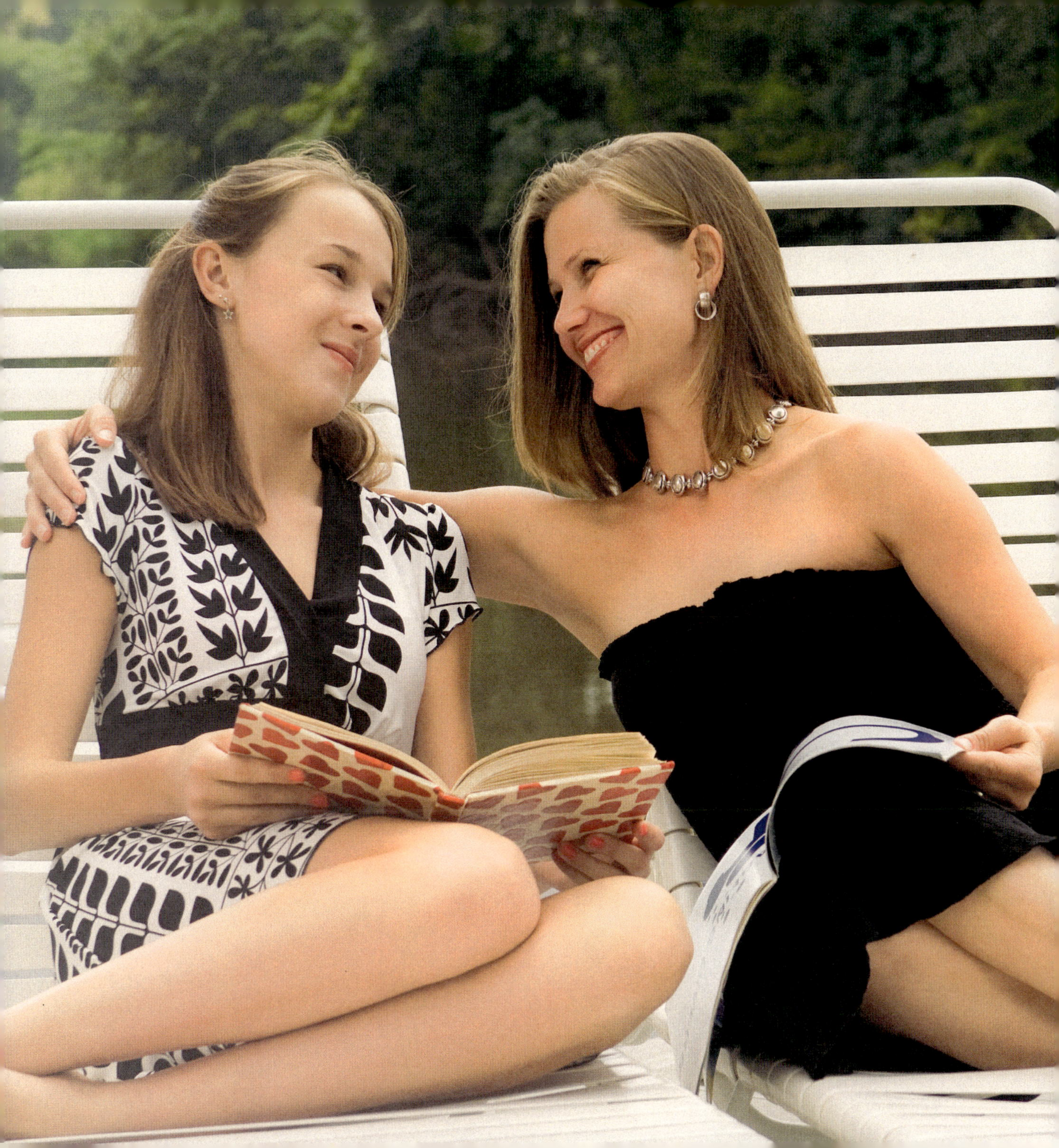

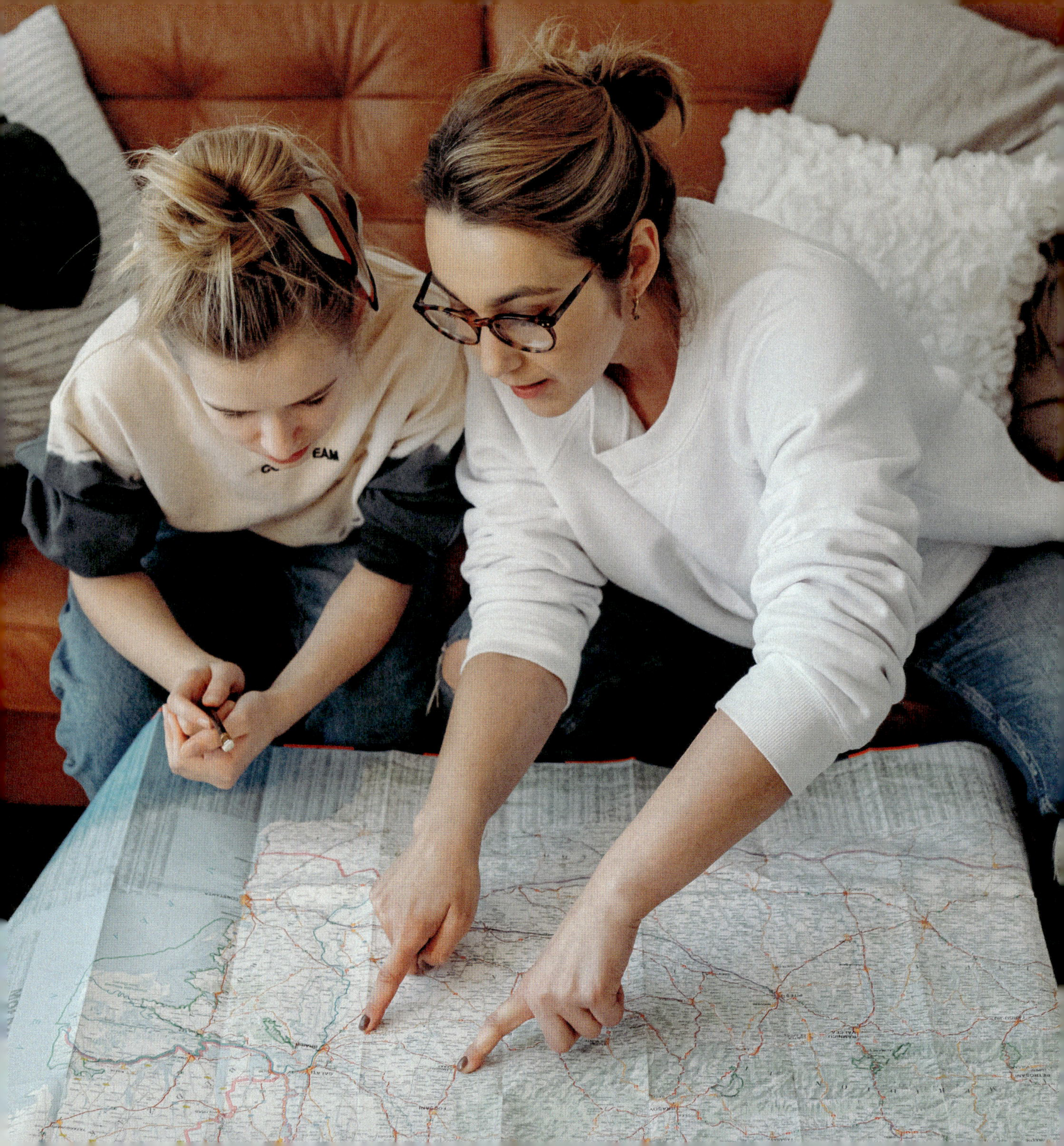

"I love my mother because she provides love and encouragement throughout my entire life and she is always there for me. She has taught me many things and I will always look up to her. I am very grateful to have her in my life."

Jane, Age 15
Lisbon, Portugal

"I love my mum because she is there for me
no matter the circumstances are.
She has an inner child like no other,
it makes her fun and bubbly.
She is funny and always makes me laugh
even when I don't want to."

Marley, Age 15
Sydney, Australia

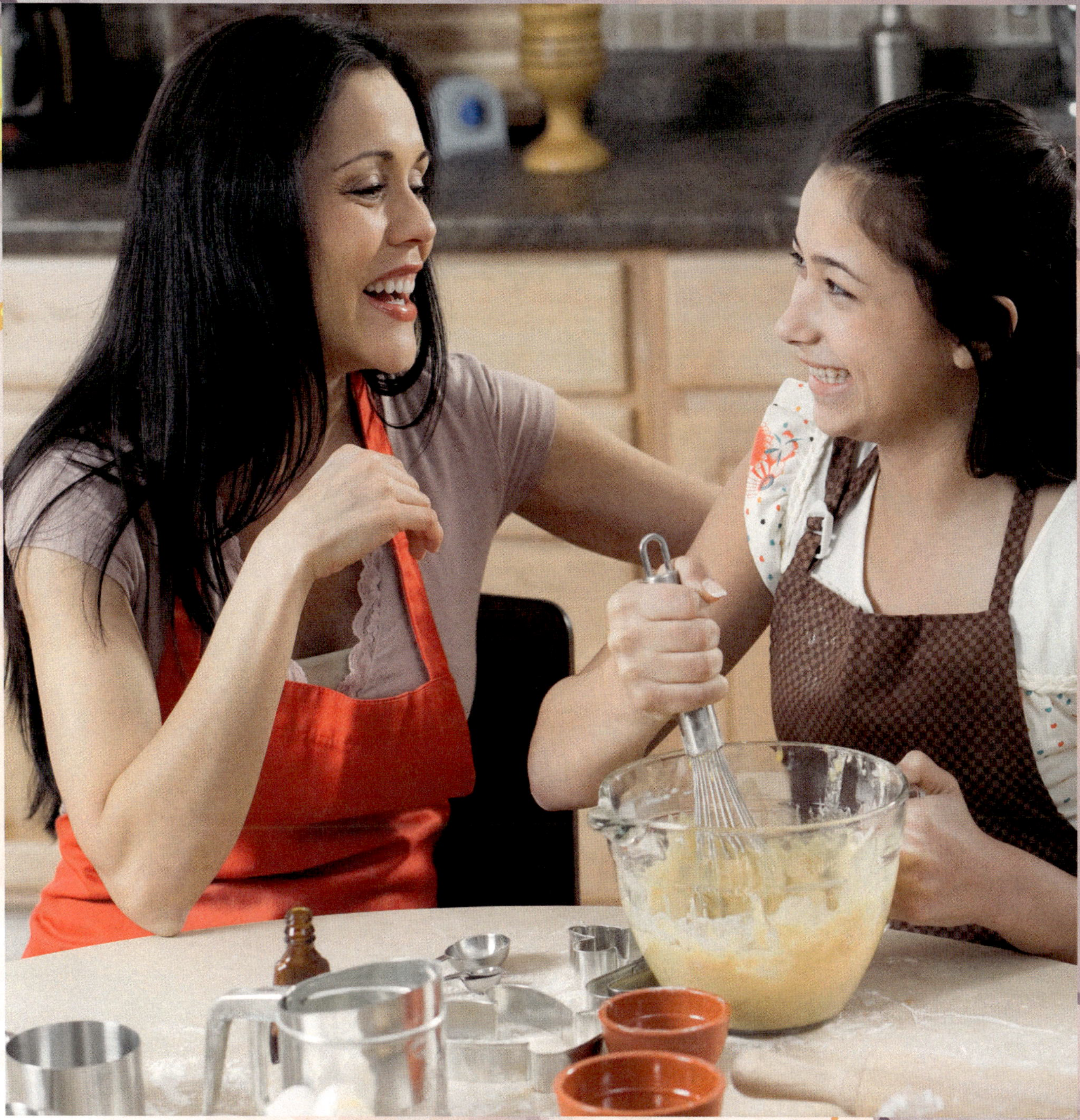

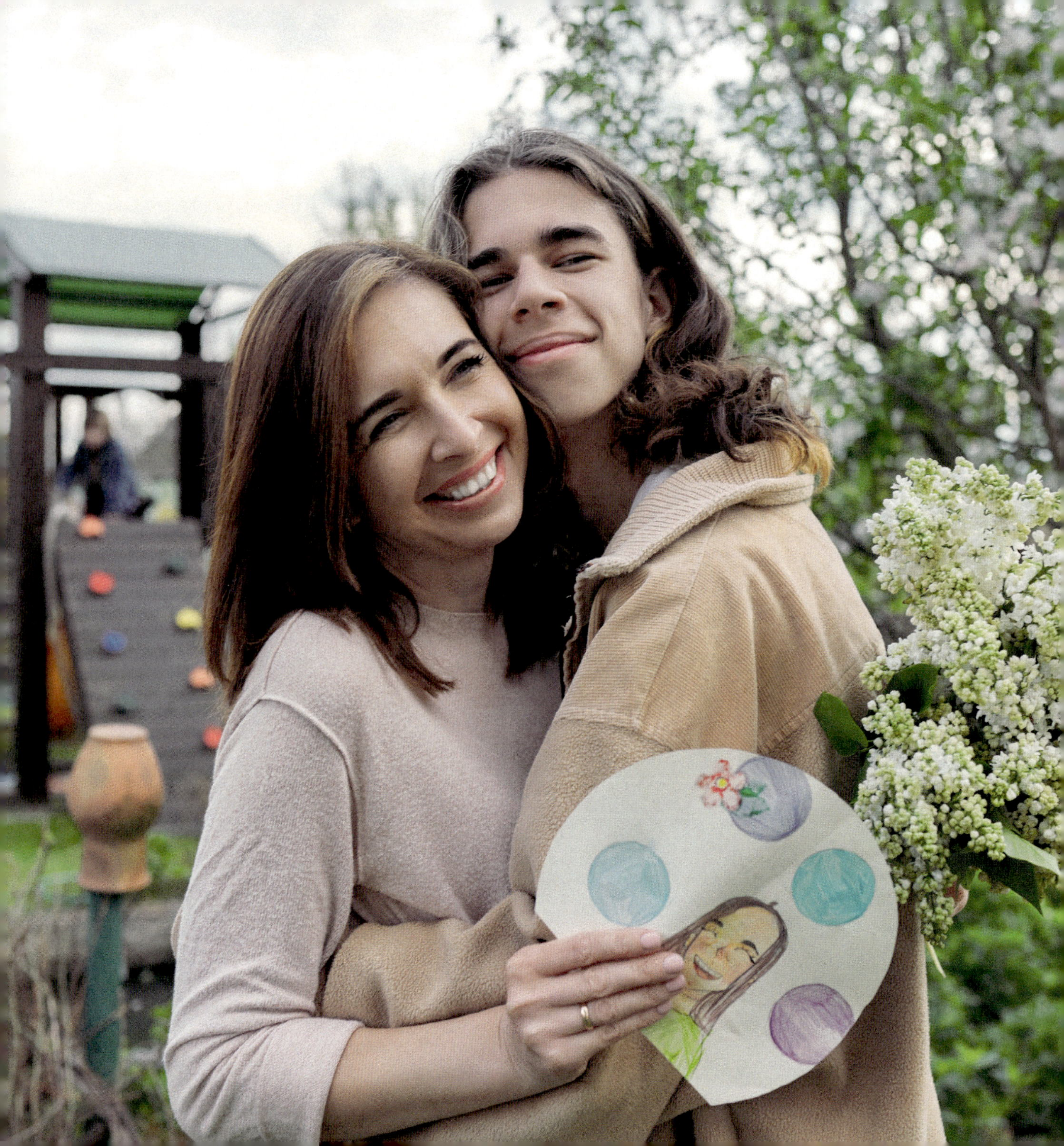

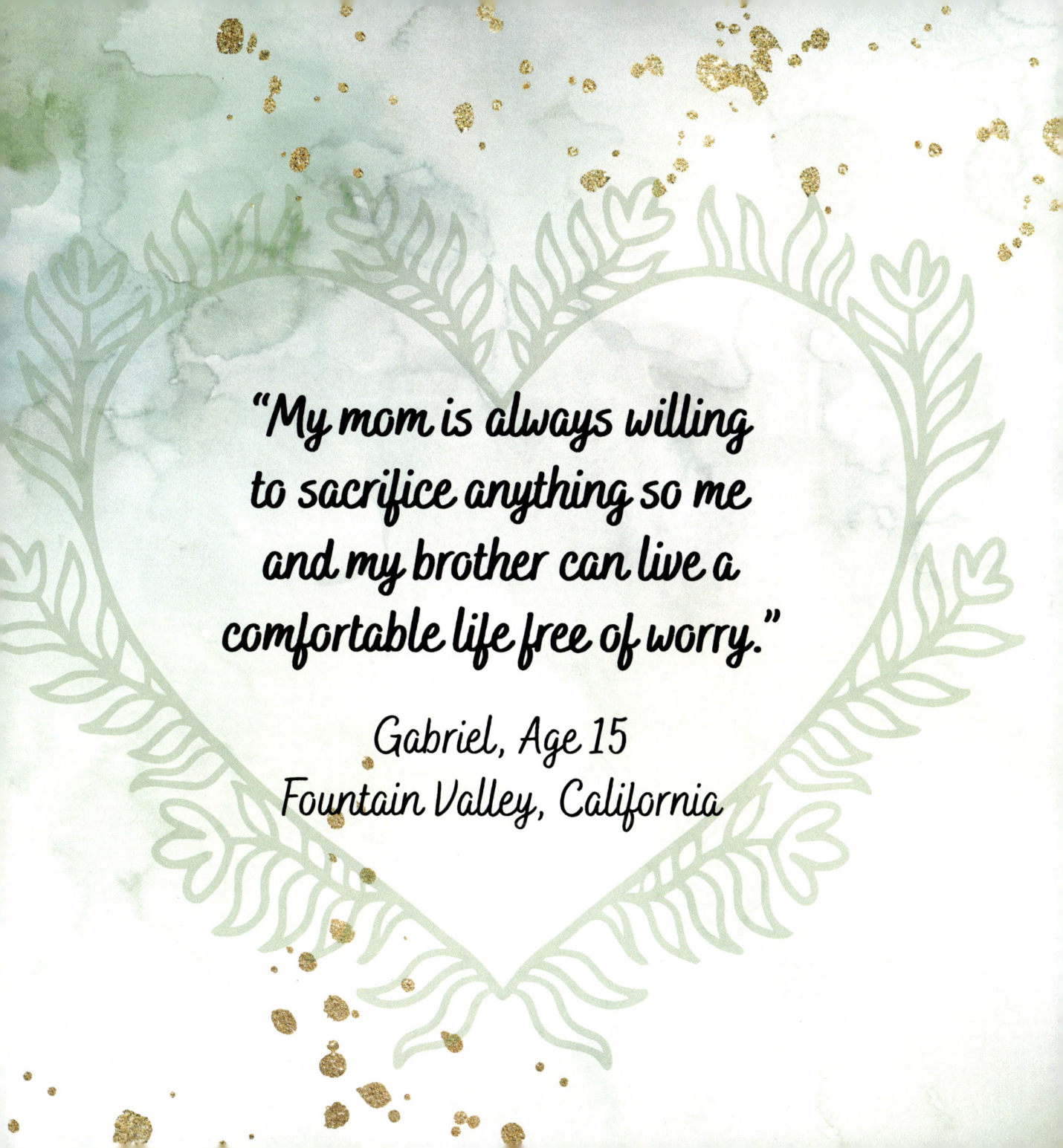

"My mom is always willing to sacrifice anything so me and my brother can live a comfortable life free of worry."

Gabriel, Age 15
Fountain Valley, California

"What I love most about my mom is that she makes a mean plate of enchiladas. She's a fun person to be around and is always trying to get us to try new things."

Keanu, Age 16
Orange County, California

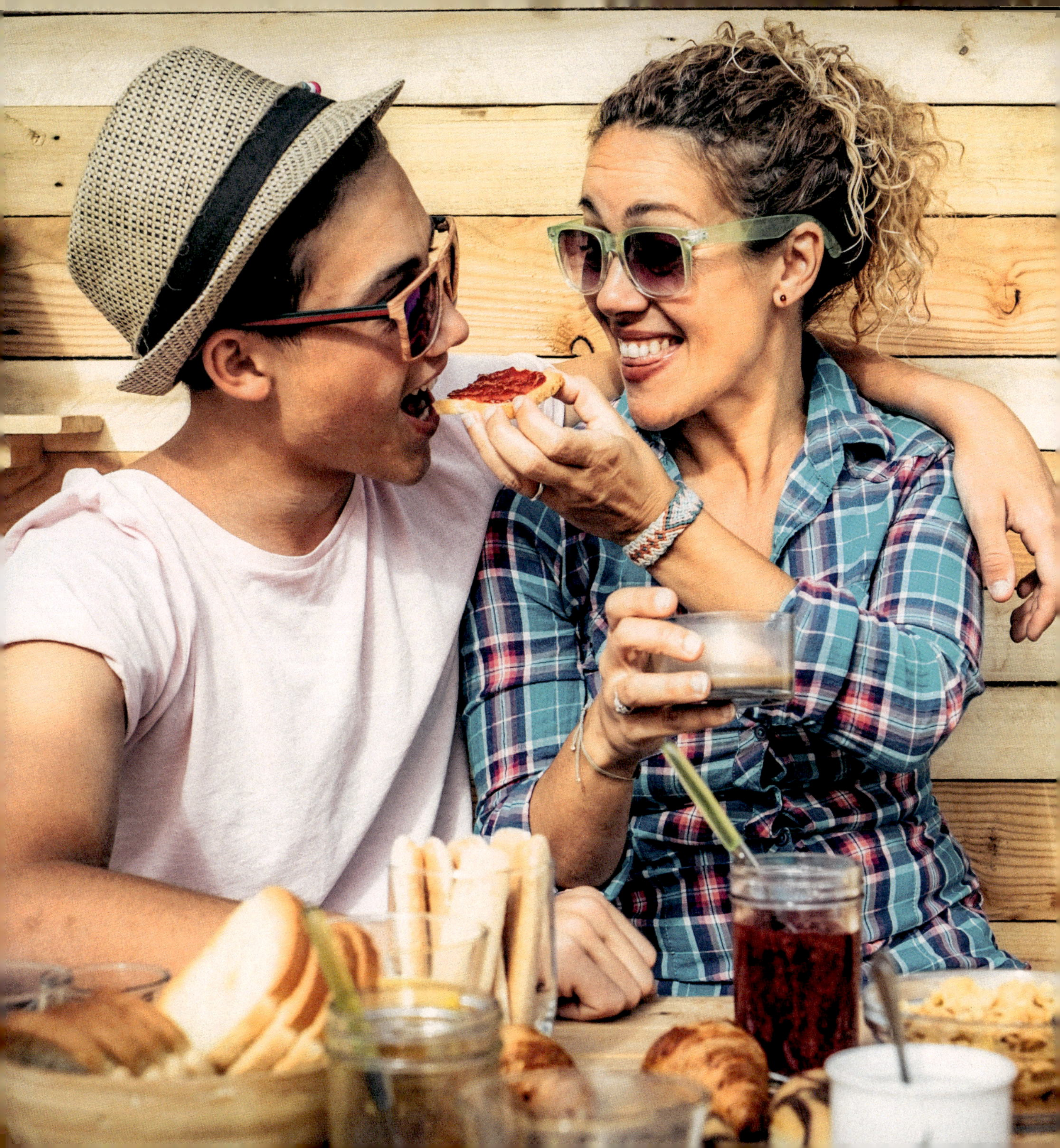

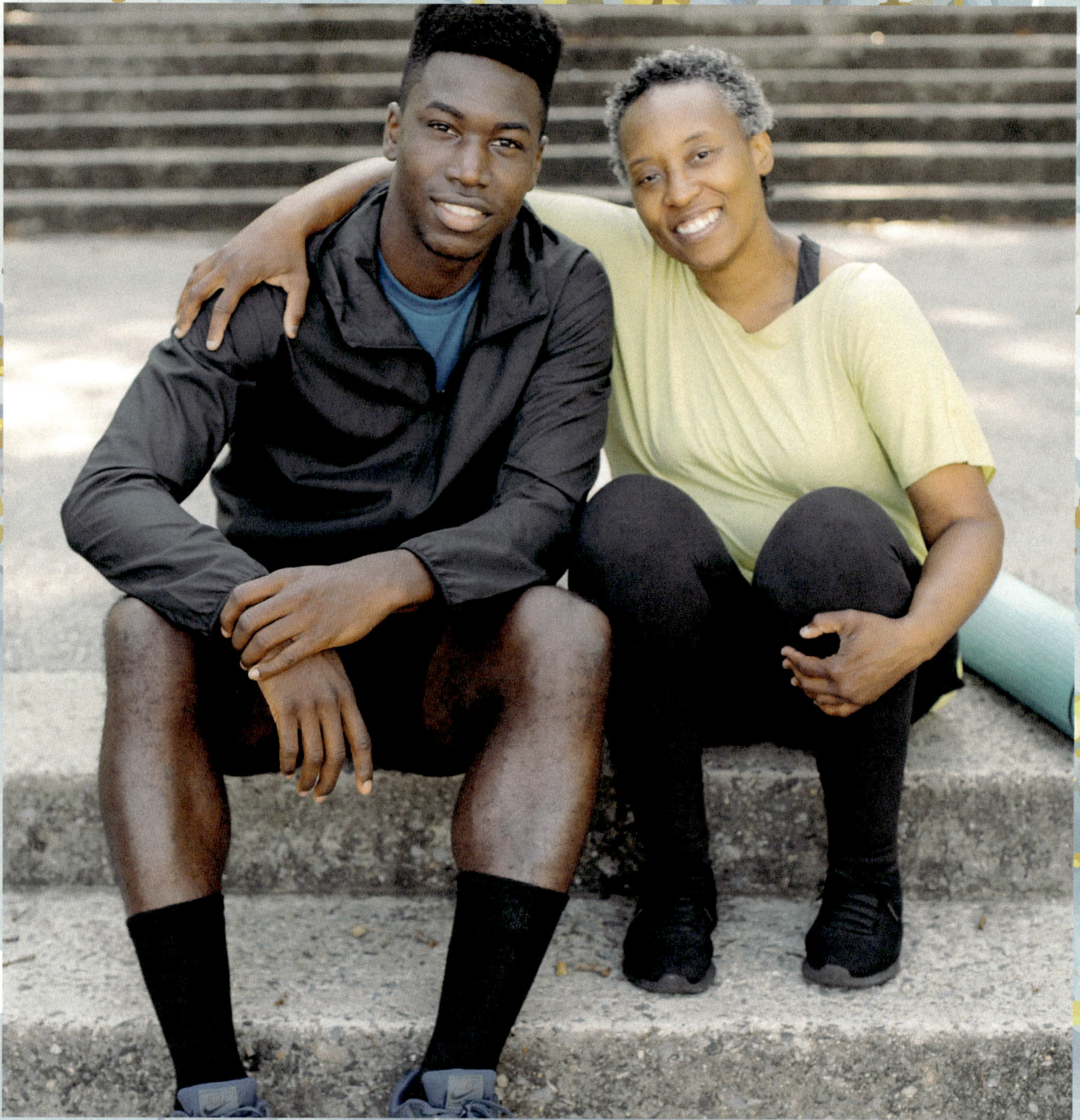

"What I love most about my mom is that no matter what situation I may be in, she will always love me."

Garrett, Age 16
West Covina, California

Acknowledgements

I would like to give a special thank you to all the parents who provided quotes from their children. Without their help, this book would not have been possible and these sweet messages of love would not be shared with the world.

Esther Davis
Candida Lottering
Lezanne Swart
Jenifer Ramona Edens
Inga Kaupelyte
Kelly Truran-Smith
Philip Shelper
Lola Edun
Alana Deegan

Caitlin Mori
Gezell Johannes
Jane Pham
Catriona Wallis
Isabel Monte
Ana Hooker
Vivienne Stein-Rostaing
Melanie de Ferranti
Kristina Drezgic
Mary Teteris

Lea Riesenman
Natalia Hooker
Sofie Flensburg Mantzar
Hannah Guix Bedford
Samantha Lyon
Egon Wong
Candice Koo
Jolinda Johnson
Julia Thomas

About the Creator of the I ♥ Mom Book:

Rachael Tarfman-Perez is the creator of the cartoon character, Gia, and the Gia Toddler-Preschool Book Series. She is also a mother of four, which is what inspired her to create her children's picture books.

As a mom, she wanted to capture the love that children have for their moms with some wonderful quotes.

www.rachaeltarfmanperez.com

- Rachael Tarfman-Perez, Children's Book Author
- rachaeltarfmanperez
- @rachael_childrensauthor
- rachael-tarfman-perez-1a9a2713
- @rachaeltarfman-perez-giasw7211

Photo Credits

#1	Mrs Vicky Altaie - Pixabay	#24	sakkmesterke - Adobe Stock
#2	Natalia Hooker	#25	Yan Krukau - Pexels
#3	mirkosajkov	#26	Ivan Samkov - Pexels
#4	5540867 - Pixabay	#27	Kindel Media - Pexels
#5	Drobot Dean - Adobe Stock	#28	RODNAE Productions - Pexels
#6	Pikwizard	#29	Lightfield Studios - Adobe Stock
#7	RebeccasPictures on Pixabay	#30	ArtwithTammy - Pixabay
#8	5311692 - Pixabay	#31	RODNAE Productions - Pexels
#9	Luongthethang - Pixabay	#32	August de Richelieu - Pexels
#10	Victoria_Watercolor - Pixabay	#33	Jupiterimages - FreeImages.com
#11	RODNAE Productions - Pexels	#34	Tran Long - Pexels
#12	alexeg84 - Adobe Stock	#35	Pixel-Shot - Adobe Stock
#13	Pavel Danilyuk - Pexels	#36	Anastsia Shuraeva - Pexels
#14	Pikwizard	#37	Alisa Dyson - Pixabay
#15	Vilandrra - Pixabay	#38	Lightfield Studios - Adobe Stock
#16	Victoria_Watercolor - Pixabay	#39	thatununes - Pixabay
#17	Pikwizard	#40	Jupiter Images - FreeImages.com
#18	Linda Mal - Pixabay	#41	Karolina Grabows - Pexels
#19	Elkaaaaaaa - Pixabay	#42	Jupiterimages - FreeImages.com
#20	Pixel-Shot - Adobe Stock	#43	Valerii Honcharuk - Adobe Stock
#21	Pikwizard	#44	Fabio - Adobe Stock
#22	Pikwizard	#45	Liliana Drew - Pexels
#23	kimberlybonioli		

Made in the USA
Columbia, SC
22 June 2023